EXERCISE YOUR MIND

Lauded in the *New York Times* for his memory training seminars, Jon Keith has been impressing people with his ability to retain information since childhood. Studying magic at the age of twelve led to his interest in the work of the great mentalists. He traces memory building back to ancient times and cultures before the written word, when stories and ideas were exchanged verbally from one generation to the next.

Jon Keith can walk into a room, meet several hundred people for the first time, and remember every person's name (his record is 644 people). He can also read a news magazine from cover to cover in an hour and tell you the contents of every page.

And now you can, too. . .

Also by Jon Keith

EXECUTIVE MEMORY TECHNIQUES

Also by Helen Tracy

GINKGO: NATURE'S BRAIN BOOSTER
(WITH ALAN H. PRESSMAN, D.C., PH.D., C.C.N.)

EVERYDAY MEMORY BUILDER

JON KEITH

with Helen Tracy

Produced by The Philip Lief Group, Inc.

BERKLEY BOOKS, NEW YORK

EVERYDAY MEMORY BUILDER

A Berkley Book / published by arrangement with
Bookspan

PRINTING HISTORY
GuildAmerica Books hardcover edition published in 2000
Berkley edition / April 2001

The Penguin Putnam Inc. World Wide Web site address is
http://www.penguinputnam.com

ISBN: 0-425-17928-1

BERKLEY®
Berkley Books are published by The Berkley Publishing Group,
a division of Penguin Putnam Inc., 375 Hudson Street,
New York, New York 10014.
BERKLEY and the "B" design
are trademarks belonging to Penguin Putnam Inc.

PRINTED IN THE UNITED STATES OF AMERICA

10 9 8 7 6 5 4 3 2 1

For Barbara

CONTENTS

Do You Need This Book?

Do you need this book? Frankly that's a no-brainer. There are as many reasons to boost your memory as there are to exercise and get your body fit. First and foremost, in both cases, you will improve the quality of your life.

Think about it. With a trained memory, you could pop out to the store and come back with *everything you went for*. Never again would you arrive home with the cereal but not the milk. Never again would you struggle to squeeze one more squiggle out of the toothpaste tube because you forgot to buy new toothpaste—for the forty-third time.

You could remember which days your daughter has soccer practice, what you bought your mother for her last birthday, and where you put your green glasses.

Or consider your life at work. You could be the one at every meeting who could present the facts of the case without searching through a stack of papers. You could remember the names of the client, her administrative assistant, her yes-man, and even her gofer. You would know, right off the top of your head, the quotes you got from four different vendors the moment your boss asked. Wouldn't that give you an edge? Wouldn't that make you look smart? Wouldn't it make you more confident?

What we learn with pleasure we never forget.

ALFRED MERCIER

You may be very intelligent, but if you can't remember what you need to, you're going to seem flaky and a little dumb. Training your memory can make your intelligence more apparent to other people. It can change the impression you make on others and it can change your image of yourself. Memory training can make you more productive and less frustrated. It can grease the wheels of life and make everything run a little more smoothly. In a nutshell, it can make your life better. Maybe a little better, maybe a lot better—but better.

But how can I tell if I have memory problems?

First of all, you don't need to have problems with your memory to profit from training. Anyone can improve on his or her natural memory.

What's natural memory?

It's what we're all stuck with. It's like your body without regular exercise—a little flabby, a little creaky, but good enough to get by most of the time. You experience the flabbiness as absentmindedness. The creakiness shows when you forget the name of the new neighbor you've met three times. And when you can't recall what you read in a newspaper article just yesterday, that's when you know you need a workout.

Here's a little test for your natural memory. Read through this list of 15 foods carefully *just once*. Concentrate on each word on the list. Then take a sheet of paper and write down as many of the items as you can remember.

mushrooms	crab	mangoes
oranges	seltzer	spaghetti
eggs	mustard	chicken
blueberries	salt	cookies
cashews	zucchini	granola

Here's how you stack up in terms of memory:

The average person 18 to 39 years old can remember ten of
the items.
Age 40 to 59, nine items
Age 60 to 69, eight items
Age 70 and over, seven items

Once you have a little memory training, you will be able to
remember all 15 items. That's a significant change.

Try another test. This time, it's something you probably do
at least occasionally. Look up a phone number you don't
know, along with the area code. Then go to your phone and
dial that number from memory. Go ahead. Look up a number
in the phone book and dial it. Then try to redial it. How many
of the ten digits did you remember? Here are the averages:

Age 18 to 39, six digits
Age 40 to 59, five digits
Age 60 to 69, four digits
Age 70 and over, three digits

How did you do? Do you have an average memory for
your age? Wouldn't you like to have a better-than-average
memory—a memory that's truly fit and in fighting trim?

**All right, I wouldn't mind having a better memory. But how
am I going to get one? I'm stuck with the brain I have.**
The brain you have is all you need. I'm no genius and I can
walk into a room, meet a hundred people, and remember
every person's name. (Actually, my record is 644 people, but
who's counting?)

**Yeah, right. And you don't just happen to have a photo-
graphic memory, do you?**
Don't have one. Not sure I'd want one. Seriously. Having a

trained memory is better than having a photographic memory. If such a thing actually exists, it's very aptly named. A photographic memory can only record—and therefore remember—what you can see. The only time this is going to help you remember someone's name is when you meet that person at a convention where everyone is wearing a little badge that reads, "Hi, my name is So and So." And face it, when everyone is wearing a name badge, you don't *need* to remember names.

Okay, you don't have a photographic memory. But you are unusually gifted, aren't you?
Not gifted. Trained. I've been training my memory for a long time. Maybe that makes me the Arnold Schwarzenegger of memory, but I started out as a ninety-pound weakling just like everyone else. Then I learned everything I could about memory training, worked on my memory skills, developed some techniques of my own, pumped a little mental iron, and ended up building a career out of helping others do the same.

Training takes time. Can't I just take ginkgo?
Take ginkgo if you think it will help, but I'll tell you right now that training takes less time and is more effective. I mean it. I have never seen anyone pop a dietary supplement and then reel off the names of 100 people they've just met. There may be long-term benefits to any number of vitamins, minerals, and herbal products. And simply being healthy is very good for your memory. The better your body functions, the better your brain functions—within limits. Physicist Stephen Hawkings's brain functions better than just about anyone's. Physical disability does not preclude genius, by any means. But good blood circulation, flexible cell walls, and a healthy supply of oxygen are all good for cognition. Still, training is the most effective memory aid anyone has ever come up with.

Memory is the treasure-house of the mind.
                                        MARGARET FULLER

Ginkgo research, for example, indicates that the supplement's antioxidant properties and its ability to improve circulation can benefit older people and those whose circulation is impaired. But there is no indication it is particularly useful to young, healthy people.

The research on memory training, on the other hand, shows that it improves memory significantly for older people and *even more* for younger people.

How long have people known about memory training?

Probably as long as people have had any kind of culture at all. After all, what did people do before they invented writing? They remembered things. The prehistoric FedEx was a fast runner with a good memory. Stories and poems weren't written down; they were *passed* down from generation to generation. In fact, poems were memory devices. The first rhyming wasn't just a way to make something sound pretty. It served a practical purpose, to make the thing easier to remember. Early poetry was probably closer to "Thirty days hath September, April, June, and November" than it was to "Shall I compare thee to a summer's day."

According to Kieran Egan, a scholar in the field of education, "If one cannot write what is in one's mind, one must remember it. If the lore of a social group is to survive a single lifetime, it must be transmitted in a stable form from generation to generation. All oral cultures place a very high value on techniques that aid faithful memorization. They rely on such techniques for their very survival. . . ."

Pulling out the big guns, are we?

That's just the beginning. According to the Greek philosopher Plato, Hermes, the man who is supposed to have invented writing, went to Pharaoh Thamus with his wonderful new technique. He said, "Look, Pharaoh, writing things down will make it possible for people to remember what they would otherwise forget." He was very proud of himself. But the pharaoh was upset. "My skillful Theut," he said, "memory is a great gift that ought to be kept alive by training it continuously. With your invention people will not be obliged any longer to train memory. They will remember things not because of an internal effort, but by mere virtue of an external device."

Sort of the way people worry now about kids using calculators instead of memorizing the multiplication tables?
Exactly. And of course, the pharaoh was wrong. People still had to remember things, especially since most people didn't learn to write until a few thousand years later. So they kept developing new memory techniques. You know all those great orators in Greece? They spoke without notes, sometimes for two or three hours.

I bet they rambled a lot, right?
Hardly. They covered every point they wanted to and nothing else. They used the "art of memory," otherwise known as *mnemonics*. According to tradition, mnemonics was invented by the Greek poet Simonides, who lived from 556 to 468 B.C. Poets were the memory experts of the ancient world. In fact, the goddess of memory in Greek mythology was the mother of the Muses, those lovely ladies who've provided inspiration to artists everywhere.

So could Simonides remember 644 names?
Funny you should ask. One night, Simonides was at a great banquet attended by hundreds of guests. During dinner, a messenger came for him and he stepped outside to receive the message. While he was outside, the banquet hall collapsed. Everyone inside was crushed, and I don't mean heartbroken. Officials needed to identify those killed and buried under the rubble, so Simonides named everyone who had been at the banquet and told the authorities where each person had been sitting. He explained that he was able to do this because he could

visualize the entire hall. With the picture fixed in his mind, he simply had to "look" at the people and name them, just as though he were in the room with them. It was a memory technique called intense visualization, something Simonides practiced all the time. In fact, he had a theory that the arts of painting, poetry, and memory were all based on intense visualization. And he was able to *teach* this technique to other people.

I could go on and on about memory training through the centuries, but don't worry, I'm not going to.

Just one more story.

Seems that in the Middle Ages, when most people still couldn't read, they came up with some mnemonic devices less sophisticated than the ones the Greeks had used. Once, a nobleman gave a certain piece of land to a monastery. To make sure that his young son would remember the transaction and honor it, he connected it with a memorable experience. He threw the boy, fully clad, into a farm pond. The boy was fished out of the pond, cold and wet, and remembered the day ever after.

Why do you know all this? I mean, how did you get interested in memory in the first place?
That's practically ancient history, too. It started when I was a kid of four. One day my parents took me to a family gathering. I was introduced to a lot of people I didn't know, and I must have found them fascinating. All I know is that I spent the whole day watching them and listening to their conversations. By the end of the day, as we were saying good-bye, I surprised the whole family by remembering everybody's name. Well, not everybody, but more than you'd expect from a four-year-old. Everyone thought I was a genius. I remembered that.

He who is not very strong in memory should not meddle with lying.

MICHEL DE MONTAIGNE

Later on, when I was ten or twelve, I didn't play ball, so I looked for other ways to impress people. I started doing magic tricks. I was pretty good at magic and folks were pretty complimentary, but I wasn't satisfied. I remembered how everyone thought I was a genius just for remembering some names, so I started studying the work of the great mentalists and incorporated it into my act. That did it. People were way more impressed with the memory feats than with the sleight of hand.

My new memory skills came in handy when I was doing my homework, too. By the time I was in college, I was teaching memory skills to other people. I even taught my own professors. And I can teach you. This book is a memory course between cardboard covers.

You're going to tell me everything I need to know in one book?

I'm going to do a lot more than tell you. If you'll work with me, I'm going to train you. Knowing the principles of the art is all well and good. But to really learn the techniques, you have to practice each one and master it before going on to the next. It's more akin to learning to play the piano than understanding the laws of physics. So I've designed this book the way I design my seminars, courses, and individual training sessions. You'll get a lot out of it even if you just read along, but you won't truly learn the techniques of modern memory training unless you work with me.

Of course, in my classes and seminars, I'm right there to cajole and encourage you through each skill. When I have a doubter—and believe me I encounter many—I can say, "Come on, just give it a try. What do you have to lose?" Usually I get the person to go with me that first step. That's almost always all it takes. After that, success takes over.

I remember a guy named Joe, from New York City. He was sort of a Tony Danza type—a little tough looking, a little tough talking. "It ain't gonna work," he told me. "Not in a million years." He kept saying that right up to the point where he had memorized lists ten and twenty items long. At that point, he changed his tune.

I'm asking you to have just enough faith to take the first step, too. Even if something seems a little odd or far-fetched to you, I want you to try the exercises.

And if it still doesn't work for me?
Go on to the next technique. There are plenty of different memory techniques in this book. Trust me, a lot of people have been working on these very methods since the days of Simonides.

Have you discovered something new about memory training? Something that old Simonides didn't know?
I know 2,500 years' worth of stuff Simonides didn't know, and the most important thing is that you learn a lot more when you're having a good time. And that's the only reason you're here, right? I needed a straight man to get things off to an entertaining start.

You're not telling me I'm fired?
I can't fire you. You're a figment of my imagination. I'm just going to unimagine you.

Oh, come on. Let me stick around. I don't have to be such a smart aleck. I can behave myself.
Sorry. You'll just get in the way from here on in.

Betcha I'll be back.
Out. I've got work to do.

All right. This is the end of the introduction. Put the book down for a bit. Go look out the window or make yourself a sandwich. Take at least a five-minute break at the end of each short chapter. You'll think better and remember more. Scoot.

PART 1

Basic Principles of Memory Training

ONE

Memory by Association

Now that you're back, let's start with an exercise, just to limber up your brain a little. And remember, if you're serious about training your memory, you should actually *do* the exercises, not just read them.

Memory Exercise #1

Take about 30 seconds and focus on the items in the following list. Then look away and write down all the items you can remember.

Pencil, Fork, Balloon, Pen, File Cabinet, Knife, Clown, Spoon, Letter Opener, Desk, Tent, Chair

How many did you remember? If you didn't do very well, you're normal. Most people will have a hard time remembering more than seven or eight of the items. Now look at the following:

Pencil, Pen, Letter Opener—items on a desk
Knife, Fork, Spoon—items in a kitchen

Balloon, Clown, Tent—items at a circus
File Cabinet, Desk, Chair—items in an office

Better? You can remember the items without much trouble because now they're organized into logical groupings. The golden rule of memory is this: If you can make material *meaningful*, you will be able to remember it easily.

You've probably heard comparisons between the human brain and computers. It's logical to ponder the similarities. However, when it comes to memory, brains and computers are different in almost every important way. First, a computer doesn't *care* whether something is meaningful. It will store and retain anything at all in its memory. And once an item is *there*, it can be retrieved.

The human brain works in quite a different way. It does not store in its permanent memory banks anything and everything that comes along. Instead, data goes first into short-term memory. It stays there briefly and then either moves into long-term memory or is discarded. If you look up a phone number, your short-term memory will usually hold onto the number sequence just long enough for you to dial it. Then *poof*, it's gone. Hours later, you won't be able to remember it, no matter how hard you try. That's because your short-term memory can hold only a handful of items, and you hadn't taken steps to store the phone number in your long-term memory.

You can alert your brain to the importance of particular information—and therefore the need to put it into long-term memory—by making that information "memorable." Most people try to do that by simply fixating on whatever it is they're trying to memorize or maybe muttering, "I've got to remember, I've got to remember" over and over, like a mantra. That won't work. Your brain will be as bored by that routine as you are. There's a better way, and it involves calling on four natural skills that you use all the time. Using these simple techniques will make your brain say, "Whooaa, baby! Here's something special."

The long-term memory seems to have a great affinity for things that can be linked, in terms of meaning, to material that's already in place. To do this, memory trainers employ *association.* And to help the brain make associations, we use *imagination, organization*, and *visualization*. These are the mental skills memory trainers use to give memory a jolt. Because that's really all you need. Your brain is going to take the information into short-term memory whether or not you make a conscious effort. What you need to do after that is, first, let your brain know you're going to want that information again and, second, find a way to retrieve it easily.

> *A man's real possession is his memory. In nothing else is he rich, in nothing else is he poor.*
>
> **ALEXANDER SMITH**

If you repeat that phone number over and over, your long-term memory will eventually lower its battlements and let the number in. But force is not the most efficient way to accomplish your aim. It is much more effective to carry out a seduction, to make your long-term memory *want* that piece of information.

Wait a minute. You're using words like "battlements" and "seduction," but what's really happening? Inside my brain, I mean.
Ask me a hard one, why don't you? Fact is, nobody really knows. People use images like computers and filing systems, words like "storing" and "retrieving," to try to explain the workings of memory. But those images and words can sometimes be misleading.

Why? Don't we store and retrieve memories?
Yes and no. Let's take a memory and look at it. Suppose you remember the first dance you had with your high school sweet-

heart at the senior prom. Perhaps you think of that memory as a little movie stashed away in a corner of your brain, but it's actually a collection of separate bits of memory. Tiny bits of that memory may be scattered throughout your brain. The music may be stored in one area, the words you spoke in another, the corsage he gave you in another. When you recall the moment, those bits all have to come together. And believe me, they don't always come together the way the moment happened in the first place.

You mean I can't trust my memory?
Well, I wouldn't go into court and testify as to what song the band was playing at the time.

"Blue Moon."
Says you. No, really. You may be right, but you could have heard "Blue Moon" in some other situation, and when your prom night memory comes together, that bit gets thrown in.

I know they were playing "Blue Moon."
Fine, fine. Don't get testy. The point I'm trying to make is that "a memory" is more like a jigsaw puzzle than a videotape. You see, we think memories are located in certain neurons in the brain. We also *think* they're in the part of the neuron called the axon, the part dedicated to communication with other cells. And there appear to be memory chains, called *memory traces*, that are linked by electrical current.

So a memory trace is like a network of wires?
Sort of. Except that the neurons in memory traces don't actually touch one another. They're separated by tiny gaps called synapses. The way we understand it right now, a thought flows from one cell to another by means of chemicals called neurotransmitters, of which there are about six that are responsible for brain function. Acetylcholine is the one that seems to be most crucial in the workings of memory.

And just how do memories get into those memory traces?
It seems to be a three-step process. First, there is *sensory register*. You look around a room and, for an instant, each thing you see, hear, smell, touch, or feel is registered by your brain. If you pay particular attention to something, like a phone number, it goes into your *short-term memory* and stays there . . . for a few seconds. Then, if nothing happens to make it stick around, it flies right out of your mind. If something does happen and your mind "decides" to keep the memory, it goes into your *long-term memory*, where it becomes, for all intents and purposes, permanent. You have learned it.

So is that why I can remember the name of the lady who lived next door when I was six but not remember whether I turned off the coffeepot?
Exactly. If you haven't "learned" something, you won't be able to remember it for long. You apparently "learned" the name of your next-door neighbor.

All right, then how do you explain how amnesiacs can remember how to read and play chess and ride a bicycle?
Well, actually there are two different kinds of long-term memory.

Aha! Gotcha!
All you've got is a habit of interrupting. I was about to say that one kind of memory is called *procedural*, and it involves "remembering how."

That's the chess-playing kind?
Yup. The other is called *declarative* memory, and it involves remembering "that."

Like "that" the capital of Illinois is Springfield?
And "that" John Adams was the nation's second president and "that" Michelangelo painted the Sistine Chapel and "that"

your name is Pat Pill, or whatever it is. Declarative memory is considerably more fragile than procedural memory. Amnesiacs lose a great deal of their declarative memory, but not their procedural memory. Now, here's the really interesting part.

I've been waiting patiently.
During the years I've been training people's memories, I've often wondered if memory theory was missing something.

How's that?
Well, look at the game of bridge. You remember "how" to play bridge, but good bridge players also remember "that" the first South led a four of diamonds and East played high from the dummy with the king, hoping that South had led away from an ace. North frustrated that hope by playing the ace of diamonds and East tossed on the six. Then, North led the ten of diamonds and East had to—

All right, all right. I get the idea. A good bridge player can remember a whole game.
Sometimes a whole tournament. Now, ordinarily psychologists and other memory researchers refer to short-term memory as "working memory" and long-term memory as "stored memory." Short-term working memory is easy to access but doesn't stick around. Long-term stored memory is permanent but needs cues for access.

Well, I started to think that there must be some kind of long-term working memory that explained bridge playing and reading and, obviously, the kinds of memory feats that I and other experts can do at the drop of a hat. I'd had this in my mind for a long time. Then, while I was working on this book, I ran across the following in a paper by psychologists K. Anders Ericsson of Florida State University and Walter Kintsch of the Institute of Cognitive Science at the University of Colorado at Boulder. They posed some interesting questions:

Can mechanisms that account for subjects' *limited* working-memory capacity in laboratory tasks also account for the greatly *expanded* working-memory capacity of experts and skilled performers? [Italics mine] . . . In this paper we propose that a general account of working memory has to include in addition to the temporary storage of information that we refer to as short-term working memory (ST-WM), another mechanism based on skilled use of storage in long-term memory (LTM) that we refer to as long-term working memory (LT-WM). . . . LT-WM is distinguished from ST-WM by the durability of the storage it provides and the need for sufficient retrieval cues in attention for access to information. (Ericsson, K.A., & Kintsch, W. (1995). Long-term working memory. *Psychological Review,* 102, 211–245.)

Are you trying to say you beat these scientists to the punch?
Not at all. I'm saying that all along, I had a vague idea that there was something missing in the way memory had been explained, and now these two experts have put their finger on it. There is a kind of memory that combines some of the qualities of both short-term and long-term memory. And that memory is what I and other memory trainers can teach you to use. Our tools are association, imagination, organization, and visualization.

First, let's consider **association**. Your brain makes associations all the time. You can't avoid it. Certain smells make you think of certain places. A particular melody will bring back an entire experience. A name can evoke emotions, pleasant and unpleasant, whose origin you can't even remember. There are probably names you don't like just because you once knew someone by that name who rubbed you the wrong way.

Second, there's **imagination**. Everyone has an imagination. Sometimes it's the source of fun, fantasy, and creativity. Sometimes it causes you to leave the light on when you're alone in the house at night. Stephen King taps into his imagination all the time, as do the people who write children's books. Most of us ignore our imaginations. But each of us has one, and we can use it to help us remember.

Third, there's **organization**. The principle of organization is used very effectively by the telephone company. Almost anyone can remember a telephone number at least for the time it takes to dial it, because the digits that make up that number are organized into smaller groupings.

Finally, there's **visualization**. Most of us don't do a lot of conscious visualization, but the "brain's eye" is one of your most potent tools, as far as memory is concerned. Your visual memory is much more efficient than your verbal memory.

Using these four skills, you can learn to remember almost anything. To begin your training, I'm going to teach you to associate two completely different objects so that whenever you think of one, you'll think of the other. Ready? Here are the objects.

SPOON   WHALE

Okay, use your imagination and your brain's eye. Come up with the most absurd, outrageous picture you can summon up to link *spoon* and *whale*. Got it?

Here are some possibilities. You could see a tiny whale swimming around in a huge spoon. You might even imagine a whole school of whales in that spoon, all spouting water like crazy. Or you could visualize a whale holding a spoon in its flippers and using it to empty the ocean. You could even picture a whale with a spray of spoons coming out of its blowhole.

Okay, have you got a picture in your mind? Now try to think about a whale without thinking about spoons. We'll pause for a moment while you give it a shot. Good luck.

PAUSE FOR THINKING ABOUT A WHALE
WITHOUT THINKING ABOUT SPOONS

Didn't do so well, did you? You've associated spoon and whale in your mind, and now it's going to be pretty hard to break that link. In fact, for the next few days, you may have a lot of whales at the breakfast table with you.

Although the spoon-whale demonstration used three of the four natural skills—imagination, visualization, and association—this was primarily an association exercise. Association is the first and foremost skill in my training program. Let me tell you a little bit about it.

Association

Association is probably the most widely used memory technique, and that's because it works. But you have to know how to use it. When someone tells you to link two things in your mind, you probably start looking for some similarity between them. When you're asked to associate *spoon* and *whale*, you might think, for example, about a spoon turned upside down on a flat surface. The shape of the overturned spoon looks a little like the contours of a whale. So you start fixating on that similarity. Wrong approach. What we're looking for here is *memorable*, remember?

> **No one is likely to remember what is entirely uninteresting to him.**
>
> **GEORGE MACDONALD**

It is interesting that what the mind finds most memorable are absurd images. (It finds images of overturned spoons resting on tables ordinary, boring, and intensely *forgettable*.) To quote Kieran Egan again, "Our tendency in educational discourse to see memorization and imagination as somewhat at odds with one another is a product of forgetting how closely tied the two processes are in our cultural history. Indeed, one might almost say that the imagination was born of the need to remember." He goes on to explain that it's no accident that myths are filled with impossible creatures performing absurd and improbable feats. That's what makes those stories memorable. And that's why, when you're doing association, you want to go for the outlandish. Think Greek myth. Think Salvador Dali. Think Monty Python. That's where your imagination comes in.

Imagination

If you're not feeling like John Cleese today, I can give you a little help. There are three techniques that stimulate your imagination—*exaggeration, switching,* and *motion.* Remember when I asked you to summon up an outrageous, absurd picture linking *spoon* and *whale*? Think about the one you came up with, and you'll see how those three things figure in.

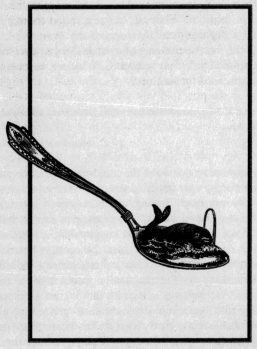

Whale in a spoon

Consider the image of the tiny whale in the huge spoon. We *exaggerated* the sizes of the objects. The whale is ridiculously small and the spoon is ridiculously large. We also *switched* the sizes of the whale and the spoon. Finally, we added *motion* when we pictured the whale swimming, spooning, and spouting.

Let's do another association, just for fun. Keep in mind the three imagination stimulators and come up with an image you'll never forget.

BOOK   PITCHER

First, use exaggeration. Think about exaggerating sizes, shapes, or qualities. What can be exaggerated about a book? What can be exaggerated about a pitcher?

All right, I came up with someone pouring a bunch of little books out of a big glass pitcher. Size is easy to exaggerate, and I guess I go for that one a lot. But that's all right. You should use the principle that you're most comfortable with. No one cares if you develop one principle over the other. I'm asking you to use all of them so that you'll discover which ones suit you best.

Okay, try switching. Think about switching the sizes, shapes, or functions of books and pitchers.

Do you have your image? I came up with a person sitting in an armchair pouring milk out of a book and reading a pitcher. I don't think this image is as good as my first one, maybe because it's a little too complicated. There are too many details besides the pitcher and the book. I may have just linked *pitcher* and *armchair* better than *pitcher* and *book*.

Finally, try making the association using motion. You can use the motions you usually think of with a pitcher or a book, but don't limit yourself to those. Another option is to use human motions, the way we did with the whale spooning the water out of the ocean. Make the objects you're trying to associate walk, run, sit, march, or dance. You can also make them fly, fall, or blow up. Remember, we're dealing with imagination and anything is possible.

 Memory Tip

If something is low in priority and high in complexity, write it down. Don't strain your memory and frustrate yourself trying to remember it.

....

Ready? The first image I came up with was a pitcher falling off a huge book and breaking. It's not bad, but I thought I could do better, so I tried again. This time, I visualized an oversized book, its cover open like a door. Little pitchers are jumping off the pages of the book and marching away from it in a line. Ridiculous? Of course—but definitely memorable.

You see, even without a whale, you can come up with memorable images. Try a few more for practice.

Memory Exercise #2

Create some memorable images, using any of the principles—exaggeration, switching, motion—you feel comfortable with, in any combination. Here are your pairs.

FEATHER	CAT
SHOE	LOLLIPOP
FISH	PICTURE FRAME
RADIO	LAWNMOWER
BANANA	CHAIR

Possible Choices

I'm going to share what I came up with, just in case you had trouble with any of these. Sometimes seeing another person's associations can help you jumpstart your own imagination.

I saw a Siamese cat curled up asleep on a big white feather that was floating down to earth.

I pictured a black wingtip shoe standing on its heel, using its "tongue" to lick a red lollipop.

I visualized a big fish mounted on the wall in a gold picture frame.

I saw an old-fashioned radio perched on a green riding lawnmower, speeding across my lawn.

I saw a large, perfectly ripe banana stretched out comfortably in a leather recliner.

Okay, pick the dud. Exactly. The fish in the picture frame is logical, predictable, and completely unmemorable. Let's replace that image with one of a big fish sitting on a pier with a fishing rod in its fins, reeling in a dripping picture frame, like the one on the next page. Much better.

You'll notice that when I describe an image, I don't just say "a fish catching a picture frame." All my sentences have very specific adjectives and verbs, like "wingtip," "old-fashioned," "float," and "stretched out." That's because I actually see these images in my brain's eye. They have reality for me, and therefore they have detail. That's where visualization comes in.

Now I want you to take a break. Put the book down, forget about fish and radios and bananas, and stretch your legs for five minutes. Don't worry—I'll still be here when you get back!

Fish with picture frame

NO SOAP!

There was once a famous actor by the name of Charles Macklin. He always bragged that he could hear a speech just once and repeat it verbatim, without a single error. He was often challenged and he often demonstrated his skill. Then, in the year 1755, Macklin boasted within hearing of playwright Samuel Foote. Foote took him up on it. He challenged the actor to repeat the following speech:

> So she went into the garden to cut a cabbage leaf to make an apple pie; and at the same time a great she-bear, coming up the street, pops its head into the shop—What! no soap? So he died and she very imprudently married the barber; and there were present the Picinnies, and the Joblillies, and the Garyalies, and the grand Panjandrum himself, with the little round button on top and they all fell to playing the game of catch-as-catch-can, till the gunpowder ran out at the heels of their boots.

Macklin had to admit that he couldn't remember the speech. It simply had too little meaning. Oddly, it turned out to be memorable in another way. We still say "no soap" to mean that something failed. And "the grand Panjandrum" is just another way to say "big shot."

TWO

Chain, Chain, Chain

Hope you had a nice walk, at least to the refrigerator. Just to see how things are going in your brain . . .

FISH

Thinking about picture frames? Good. Now we can go on with the association work. The next step is to associate more than just a pair of things. We're going to go for a half dozen:

SWAN
GUITAR
TENT
COIN
BUG
DESK

The obvious approach is to try to come up with some sort of visualization that includes all six objects—a swan sitting in a tent playing a guitar next to a pile of coins and bugs and . . . Oh dear, what about the desk? Let me start over. A swan sitting on a desk in a tent playing a guitar next to . . . This is not working. The idea is to make things memorable, not confusing. For the average brain, when you get above three or four items, that means *sequence*.

Sequence

According to my handy unabridged dictionary—used most often in our house for Scrabble games—a sequence is "a series having continuity and connection." A numerical sequence can be "1,2,3,4,5 . . ." or "2,4,16,256. . . ." (In the second case, each number is the square of the one before.) An alphabetical sequence could be "apple, ball, cat, dog, elephant, foot." A timeline presents a chronological sequence.

1776—The Declaration of Independence is signed.
1777—The Articles of Confederation are signed.
1781—Cornwallis surrenders at Yorktown.

The plot of a story presents another kind of chronological sequence. "And then the bad guy jumped into the river and then he climbed up in a boat and then he pulled his gun out and then he tried to shoot it and it wouldn't go off. And then . . ."

For some reason, the human mind really likes sequences. It will remember hundreds of pieces of information if it can find some kind of sequence in them, such as the plot of a story. But what if you have a bunch of things to remember and they don't seem to have any built-in sequence? Easy. You create one. The important thing is that each item in the sequence must be connected to the item before it and to the item after it *and only to those two items*. In other words, you want a chain. Let's look at those six items again:

SWAN	COIN
GUITAR	BUG
TENT	DESK

Obviously, you can start with a swan playing a guitar. It's easy, it's silly, and it's memorable. Now forget about the swan for a moment. Focus on the guitar and the tent. What can you do with a guitar and a tent?

I came up with a huge guitar, big as a mountain, and a little campsite pitched right on top of it. I really am partial to those size exaggerations. Another possibility is a circus tent with guitars in clown costumes tumbling over each other in the center ring.

Whatever you came up with, think about it for a few seconds and then forget the guitar for the time being. Now you're dealing with a tent and a coin. What about a circus tent with banners flying and bright gold coins spilling from every entrance, as in the picture on the next page? Think about it for a moment or two. It takes a few seconds for something to register in your long-term working memory. Now on to the bug. Coin and bug. See yourself counting out bright red ladybugs from a little coin purse, the kind with a metal clasp that snaps shut. Think of that image. See it in your mind. Then drop the image and go on to bug and desk. A big ladybug this time, sitting at a fancy Victorian writing desk.

Now, just to set the sequence, look at the list and say the six words *out loud*. I'm serious. If there's someone else in the room as you're reading this and you're embarrassed to talk out loud, step into the bathroom and do it there. As you say the six words, deliberately summon up the images you created.

Okay now, cover the list and see if you can remember the six items.

Circus tent with coins

NO TURNING BACK TO PEEK.

How'd it go? Were you able to remember all six items? Did you recall them in sequence? Did you need to use the images you had come up with?

If the answer to the last question is "No," everything is normal. The images are necessary to make the connection between one item and the next and register each item in long-term memory. Once the connection is there, the image has outlived its usefulness. Most of the time, it will simply disappear. You will probably be able to recall it if you try, but you won't need it to remember the item. Trust me on this one.

Memory Exercise #3

Here's another item group for you. Remember, you want a sequence, a *chain* of information:

AIRPLANE
CIGARETTE
WINDOW
MOOSE
CAR
PAN

Keep in mind the imagination stimulators we talked about in chapter 1—exaggeration, switching, and motion. Be sure to hold each image in your mind a few seconds before you go on to the next image. Don't go back to any previous image when you're coming up with a new one. Review the images by saying the words aloud. Then try to remember the words in sequence.

Possible Choices

All right, here are my images for those words. For *airplane* and *cigarette* I pictured a cartoon airplane with a big face on the nose, smoking a cigarette, with smoke rings rising like clouds. For *cigarette* and *window* I imagined a big cigarette crawling through a window like a burglar, looking around to make sure nobody's home. For *window* and *moose* I saw a moose with a window fitted into his side so that you could look right through him. For *moose* and *car* I pictured a moose cruising along in a convertible, antlers whistling in the wind, as in the picture on the next page. Then for *car* and *pan* I saw a huge frying pan with a stock-car race going on inside it, cars whizzing around and driving up the sides.

Moose in car

Memory Exercise #4

Now here's a list for you to do on your own. I'm not going to give you any possible choices. Just let your imagination go to work. It can be very helpful to think in terms of cartoons, because the more outrageous or ridiculous the image, the more memorable it will be. Think of Saturday mornings spent in front of the television with Daffy Duck and Bugs Bunny. For inspirational purposes, Looney Tunes are the best. To limber up your mind for this exercise, think of Daffy getting his tail feathers blown off in an explosion, the Roadrunner going through solid rock and leaving a hole just his shape in the cliff, Sylvester flattened by a falling safe, and Yosemite Sam shooting up the town. These are your muses. Now go to work:

BICYCLE
OSTRICH
VASE

KITE
FENCE
WALRUS

That's just about enough work for right now. But if you're wondering what good it's going to do you to be able to associate swans and guitars or ostriches and bikes, let me explain.

This skill is extremely useful in all kinds of memory situations. For the moment, you're just getting the hang of it, but later you'll be using variations on this skill for remembering the names and faces of people you meet at parties or business meetings. It will bear on our work in remembering appointments and numbers, telephone and otherwise. And in the meantime, you can use association to remember what you need to take to an appointment or pick up at the grocery store or pack for an overnight stay.

So why don't you do one more list before you take a break?

Ostrich on bike

Memory Exercise #5

This time, there will be no swans or walruses, just a few things you might want to take with you when you go to visit your Aunt Eulalie, who lives near the beach. (I *know* you don't have an Aunt Eulalie. Neither do I, as it happens. I'm using mnemonic license.) We'll assume you can remember to pack your underwear.

CAMERA
VITAMINS
SWIMSUIT
TOOTHBRUSH
GIFT
BOOK
SANDALS
BANK CARD
CELL PHONE

Ready, set, visualize! Then go fly a fence.

MAKE YOUR OWN MOVIE

If you have a little faith in your imagination and are the verbal type, you might want to try a different kind of sequence. As I pointed out before, your memory loves a good story. Or rather, it loves a good plot. Details may easily fall by the wayside. So, confronted by a list to commit to memory, you can always create a movie plot. As usual, the more outrageous—and the more visual—the better. Here's a list of words I got by opening the dictionary at random:

CRAB	HOLLY	BRIDGE
TILE	PULLEY	FLASK

—and the mini-movie plot I came up with to remember them.

The camera pulls back to reveal a giant **crab** holding a **holly** tree over a river to form a **bridge**. The bed of the river is **tiled** with orange ceramic tiles. Suddenly a helicopter flies in from nowhere and hovers over the crab, lowering a **pulley**. The crab drops the tree and grabs the pulley. As the helicopter flies away, the crab climbs up the pulley rope and the pilot hands it a **flask**, from which it takes a big swig.

Okay, cover the page and try to remember the six words. Did you remember all six? If you didn't, I'll bet you forgot *tile*. It was part of the detail of the story, not the plot.

THREE

What's in a Name?

I hope you used your break to watch Bugs outwit Elmer Fudd, because you're going to put your visual imagination to good use in this session. We're about to tackle a skill that is valuable to just about anyone in just about any situation. I'm about to teach you how to remember names.

Faces are easy, of course. Just about everybody remembers faces. Faces are, after all, visual images. That very efficient visual memory of ours latches onto them and stores them away with ease. A study done in the mid-1970s shows just *how well* we remember faces. Test subjects were shown five faces from yearbooks dating back to their high school years. They were asked to choose the one person of the five they had actually been to school with. Even people who had been out of school for 35 years were able to pick out their schoolmates 90 percent of the time! It didn't matter that they had met thousands of people in the intervening years. And it didn't matter how large their graduating class had been. The results were the same for those who had been one of a hundred and those who had been one of seven or eight hundred.

Putting names to faces is an entirely different matter. In the same study, people who were out of school only three months could put names to the faces of only 15 percent of their classmates. People who had been out of school for 40 years could remember only 9 percent of the names.

There's a story about the famous British conductor, Sir Thomas Beecham. One day in the early part of the twentieth century, he found himself in the lobby of a hotel in Manchester, England. He saw a very distinguished woman whom he was quite sure he knew. Unfortunately, he couldn't remember her name. She seemed to recognize him as well, however, so he stopped to chat with her. He had a vague memory that she had a brother, so thinking he might get a clue to her identity, he asked how her brother was. "Is he still working at the same job?" Beecham probed. "He's very well . . . and still king," said the woman, with a slightly startled expression.

Every single one of us has been in that same situation, although most of us aren't personally acquainted with royalty. It may be funny in the retelling, but it's almost always embarrassing at the time, not to mention mildly insulting to the person whose name you can't remember. It can be a serious problem if the person is a client you've been hoping to land for your firm. It's almost as serious if he's the husband of your supervisor, and you'd met him at dinner only a couple of months before. It usually turns out to be a nice person whose feelings you don't want to hurt.

If you have trouble remembering names, a business meeting where you meet more than one or two people may very well be a nightmare for you. The thought of walking into a room, shaking hands, and then trying to hold six new names in your head could send those sweat glands into overdrive.

> *I sometimes worry about my short attention span, but not for very long.*
>
> **HERB CAEN**

Well, you're about to take the first step toward becoming Ruler of the Name Domain. From now on, you will remember not only the account executive but also the receptionist, the security guard, and anyone else who crosses your path.

In fact, your first task for this session is to imagine what your life is going to be like when you can remember the name of every person you meet. I don't know anything about your life, so you have to fill in all the blanks yourself, but just sit there for a moment and think about it. Are your days on the job going to go more smoothly? Are you going to be less nervous at your high school reunion? Will running for president of your neighborhood improvement association become a real possibility? As I said, I don't know your circumstances, but you do. Imagine.

The reason I'm asking you to do this is that positive expectations have a huge impact on your ability to remember. In fact, you can probably improve your memory 5 to 10 percent *just* by being positive. In one recent study, two groups of people were tested on memory skills. One group was told that they could improve their memories, and the other wasn't. With no other difference between the two groups, those who believed they could improve scored significantly higher on the tests. When you combine a positive attitude with the memory skills you're learning now, the result will be pretty amazing. Seriously. It will.

Okay, let's get started. The first step in the name game is to—guess what?—turn the name into a visual image. That's why we've been doing all the exercises in the first two chapters—so we could apply these skills to practical tasks, such as remembering names.

Memory Exercise #6

To begin, I'm going to give you a list of last names that I picked at random from a telephone book, going from A to Z. You're going to try to come up with a visual image for each of them.

Obviously, this is going to be a little more challenging than coming up with a visual image for an object. There are a few names that conveniently refer to objects as well as people—names like Stone, Singer, Ball, Hill, Frost, Banks, Baker, Elder, and Tower. Then there are names that are also descriptive terms, like Stout, Long, and so forth. But most names don't have obvious meanings. You're going to have to do some playing around with sounds, the way you might if you were playing charades. Loosen up. Are you ready?

AGARD
BITTING
CORRAL
DAUGHERTY
FERRANTE
GONSOWSKI
HOLLOWELL
JACKSON
LOFTUS
MONAHAN
PAROLA
RAMIREZ

Possible Choices

All right, the first name is Agard. Just guessing at the way it's pronounced, I'll choose the image of a bank guard. You know, a guy in a uniform, with a gun at his hip, standing next to a bank vault.

Next is Bitting. Looking at this name, I might come up with something that has to do with biting. But I wouldn't be looking at the name if I were meeting this person. I'd be hearing it, and I think what I'd hear would sound a lot like "bidding." So I'm going to go with somebody at an auction holding up one of those little paddles that means you're bidding on an item.

Corral is easy. It's one of those names that is also a thing. I'm seeing a mental picture of the gunfight at the O.K. Corral, but if you're more of a pacifist, you might see someone training a horse in a corral or just a corral, empty and dusty in the hot sun.

Daugherty. Again, looking at it makes me want to go with daughter, but I know the name is pronounced *DOR'tee*. So I'm going with a door with a big capital letter *T* on it. And with Ferrante, I think I see an auntie—a pleasant middle-age woman—in a fur coat. A fur auntie.

 Memory Tip

To remember whether you locked the door, look at your key in the lock for a full second before taking it out.

··

Gonsowski is not a name you'll run into every day. When my finger landed on it in the phone book I was tempted to try again. But I'm playing fair here, so I left it on the list. And once I said the name to myself, I was glad I did. Try saying it out loud. Hear that? I'm going with "gone south to ski" and I'm seeing a waterskier in the Florida Everglades.

Getting the hang of this now? If so, the next one is a piece of cake. Hollowell. Hollow well, right? I see a wishing well with an echo. And Jackson? I'm picturing a grown-up Jack on his way up the beanstalk with his six-year-old son right behind him.

Loftus? My honey and me, we're sitting on a loft bed with our feet dangling over. Monahan? Oops, this one is a little harder, for me anyway. I want to do this fast, so I'm going with "money hand." A hand filled with money. At least it's a memorable image. I mean, I never have trouble remembering money. And not every image is going to be a zinger. It'll work, just the same.

Parola. All right, I'm going to throw you a curve. The word that comes right into my mind is Victrola. I know it's really different from the name Parola. But it's what came first, and I trust that. It's a very easy image to remember. And it's a pretty good sound match, even if it begins differently. But you might want to go with something that has to do with "payroll." Or if you remember the sixties, there's always "payola."

Ramirez. I think "rub mirrors." I see a magician rubbing a mirror to produce an illusion.

Got the idea? Good. Of course, when you're introduced to someone in real life, you're going to have to come up with an association in a matter of seconds. There won't be enough time to mull things over and come up with the very best image. Speed is more important than quality. Go with the first image that springs to mind. All you really want, after all, is some instant association that will stir up your memory.

Memory Exercise #7

If you've got an egg timer, set it for one minute, and do this list as fast as you can:

BOSTIC
CARNEY
EISENHART
GOLDMAN
HUBERT
LERNER
MARTINEZ
MOLONEY
PETROVIC
RUSSELL
TANNER
WYDER

Possible Choices

Did you have some fun with these names? Okay, here's what I came up with:

Bostic	boss stick (cartoon boss stuck to the wall)
Carney	carny (carnival worker)
Eisenhart	eyes and heart
Goldman	gold man (Academy Awards statuette)
Hubert	hue burp (someone belching a rainbow)
Lerner	learner (a student at a desk reading a book)
Martinez	tea nest (a nest with a tea bag in it)
Moloney	bologna
Petrovic	pet roving (a lost dog)
Russell	rustle up some grub (a cowboy cook at a campfire)
Tanner	sun tanner
Wyder	wider (someone wider than the doorway he's trying to walk through)

If you did the list quickly, your associations are probably no more brilliant than mine. But that's not important. You're not getting graded on the quality of your associations, and no one is ever going to know what they are but you. If you meet Mr. Martinez and can't think of anything that sounds like the whole word but "tea nest" works for you, then that's fine. As you get more practice with this technique, your skills will become sharper and your images will become more apt.

Okay, you've just used the visualization skills you developed in chapter 1. Now you're going to use the info-chaining you learned in chapter 2. Why? Because most people have two names.

Yes, indeed, you are about to visualize a first name and then chain it to a last name. I'm not going to insist you take a break yet, but if you've been working for fifteen minutes, you should take a five-minute break. That's a very good rule of thumb. Fifteen minutes on and five minutes off. I'll be here when you get back.

Memory Exercise #8

Okay. First, let's go over some first names. I'll go back to the handy telephone book and pick a few at random:

PATRICK
SIMONE
ROGER
CARLA
FRANK
JEAN
RICHARD
SHERRI
SOLOMON

Possible Choices

Let's see. For Patrick, I come up with "hat trick," which in soccer and hockey means three goals in one game. So I'm seeing a soccer player kicking a goal into the net. Simone gives me "sea moan." That's a person leaning over the railing of a ship, moaning with seasickness. Roger makes me think of a maharajah. Carla is, of course, a car. Frank is a frankfurter. Jean is a pair of jeans.

Richard is a good example of how images can be personalized. For a friend of mine, Richard is and always will be Shakespeare's King Richard III, lying on the battleground with one arm up in the air, crying "A horse, a horse, my kingdom for a horse." It's a very strong image, and it flashes into her mind every time she hears the name Richard. It would be flatly silly for her to use any other image. On the other hand, people who are less literary would never link the name Richard to an image of a guy yelling for a horse. Personally, I just go with a rich guy.

Sherri will probably bring to mind a cherry. Solomon might make you picture the towering biblical figure—or, if you're hungry, you might think "salmon" first.

Memory Exercise #9

All right, quickly now. Set your egg timer and do this list in one minute:

CARMEN
DAVE
EDDIE
BONNIE
BARBARA
CHRIS
STEVE
MICHAEL
AMY
ARLENE

Possible Choices

Carmen	car full of men
Dave	date (calendar page)
Eddie	eddy (small whirlpool)
Bonnie	bonnet
Barbara	bar
Chris	crisp (potato chip)
Steve	steam
Michael	microphone
Amy	aiming (rifle)
Arlene	a leaning "R"

Now here's the good news. Once you've decided on an image that works for a particular name, you can use it over and over again. So since every other person you meet is named Michael, this whole memory thing is like falling off a log, swimming downstream, spitting with the wind . . . you get the idea.

Want to try one more? What image comes to mind when you hear the name Bobby Cookson? Check below for my visual one. Remembering names does not have to fill you with anxiety. It can be a lot of fun.

Now go take a nap.

Here's what I might imagine when introduced to "Bobby Cookson."

Maybe it's because actors give their memories a lot of exercise, but many anecdotes about memory seem to have actors in the leading role. The legendary Irish American actor James Cagney—Jimmy to his friends—had a phenomenal memory. In a 1984 interview in *Parade* magazine, when Cagney was 85 years old, his wife bragged a little about it:

> One day not long ago, we were getting into the car in New York, and Jimmy saw a man across the street.
> "You see that fellow over there?" he said to me. "He sat next to me in school. His name is Nathan Skidelsky."
> "Prove it," I told him. "Go say hello." So he did. And you know what? It was Nathan Skidelsky. The only problem was, he didn't remember who Jimmy Cagney was.

Now, that's a problem I can't solve.

 ## The 1-2-5 Memory Method

Here's a little memory shortcut that will come in handy in all kinds of study and learning situations. The *first* day you are exposed to new material you want to remember, review it once. It doesn't matter if the material is in print form or you've heard it in a lecture or business presentation; review the content (reread it or go over your notes) just one more time *on the same day*. Repeat the review on the next, or *second*, day and again on the *fifth* day. By that time, you should have learned the material.

FOUR

Ready-to-Wear Name Images

Reinventing the wheel is one of life's great time wasters. You need images to go with names. I've been coming up with images to go with names for a couple of decades. So I'm going to give you some lists of my images, straight off the rack. DON'T memorize them. Just look them over. You may find yourself using these very images when you meet people. Then again, you may not. If they click with you, great. If they don't, you'll come up with your own. I'm not going to elaborate on the images. I'm just going to give you one or two for a springboard. For example, take the name "Ada—first aid." The image for Ada could be a white first-aid kit with a big red cross on the lid. On the other hand, you might visualize someone administering CPR. The idea is to use the first image that pops into your head when you see the words "first aid."

One reason I'm providing these ready-to-wear images is to reinforce what I said about coming up with the perfect image. You don't have to. Don't waste your time. Your image for a particular name is nothing more than a nudge you give your memory. No one else will ever know what it is. Sometimes you might come up with an association so clever you'll wish you could tell everyone, but that isn't the point of the exercise. The point is to remember the name. These images help me remember these names. Some of them may seem odd to you. Fine. If I were completely normal, would I have this job?

Right. First names first. At the core of these lists are the 50 most common women's and men's names in the United States, among all ages, according to the 1990 census. I've added some of the nicknames that go with these names and then included many other names that I've run across in my years of conducting seminars and presentations on memory enhancement. The last list is based on the 50 most common last names, according to the census. Then I added a bunch more I thought we could have some fun with.

What I'd like you to do first is look at Part I of the women's list. Read it through once, visualizing each image. Is "aim E" a hunter aiming a rifle at a great big *E*? Or perhaps a target shooter aiming a great big *E* at a target? Fix the image for each name in your mind. Then go back and read the list through again to reinforce the associations. Then take a break. Do not go on to the next list. Take a break. Do not go back to read through the list once more to see what you remember. TAKE A BREAK.

FEMALE NAMES (PART I)

Abby—a bee
Ada—first aid
Agnes—a nest
Aisha—eraser
Alberta—all birds
Alice—a glass
Amanda—a man
Amy—aim E
Angela—angel
Ann—hand
Anna—hand her
Ashley—ash
Barbara—bar

Bella—bell
Betty—bed
Blanche—branch
Brenda—bender
Brooke—brook
Camille—a meal
Candace—can of lace
Carla—call her
Carol—Christmas carol
Caroline—carry a line
Carolyn—carry lint
Catherine—cat ring
Christine—pristine
   Chris—crystal
   Tina—team
Courtney—court room
Cynthia—cinder
Dawn—dawn
Deborah—debutante
   Debbie—dead bee
Debra—debutante
Diane—dying hand
Dolores—door for us
Donna—donut
Dorothy—door
Eileen—I lean
Eleanor—L on a door
Elizabeth—lizard
   Beth—bath
   Betty—bed
Ellen—L in
Erica—error
Fay—fade
Frances—France
   Fran—fan
Gladys—glass

Harriet—hairy
Heather—feather
Helen—heel in
Hilary—the hill
Ingrid—in red
Irene—my ring
Isabel—is it a bell?
Jackie—jockey
Jane—chain
Janet—jam in a net
Janice—jam on ice
Jennifer—gem fur
Jessica—jettison
Joyce—juice
Juanita—egg beater
Justine—just tea

First time through? Go back over the list. Second time through? Make yourself a sandwich. Take a walk around the block. Sit by the window and daydream. Do the dishes that are sitting in the sink. Wash out your favorite shirt by hand. Do anything at all except continue to work.

I MEAN IT.

I know that some of you didn't take a break. You figure that if working a little is good, then working longer and harder is better. I'M the expert, but YOU know better. I've spent most of my life learning how to put things into a brain so that they can be retrieved easily and accurately. I've learned that when you study, you should take a five-minute break just about every fifteen minutes. That's why this book is written in short chapters, to help you learn the material more easily. Trust me. I have your best interests at heart.

Anyway, go through part II of the women's name list the same way.

Take a nap.

FEMALE NAMES (PART II)

Karen—carrot in
Kathleen—cat leaning
    Kathy—cat E
    Kate—cake
Kimberly—timber
Laura—law
Lee—a lead
Linda—lint
Lisa—lease
Mabel—marble
Marcy—mars see
Margaret—Mars net
    Meg—keg
    Maggie—mag wheels
Maria—mare
Marie—marry
Martha—martyr
    Marty—more tea
Mary—marry

Megan—egg on
Melissa—kiss her
Michelle—my shell
Millie—mill
Nancy—fancy
Nicole—nick coal
Pamela—family
   Pam—pan
Patricia—Pat's richer
   Pat—pat
Paula—pull
Phyllis—fill this
Rebecca—backer (money)
Ruth—root
Sandra—sand her
Sarah—say "rah" or sharer
Sharon—sharing
Sheila—shield
Shirley—curly
Stella—cellar
Stephanie—step on me
Susan—sue her
Teresa—terrace
   Terry—terry cloth
Tiffany—Tiffany lamp
Tracy—trace
Valerie—valley
Vicky—victory (the *V* sign)
Viola—viola
Virginia—virgin
   Ginny—gin E
Wanda—wander
Wendy—windy
Whitney—whip
Wilma—will her
Winona—granola

Yvonne—she on
Zelda—sell her
Zoe—sew E

If you've been through the list once, go back to the beginning and read it through again. If you've been through it twice, you know what to do, don't you?

Go fishing.

Back from your break? Great. Now, go through the list of men's names in the same way. Visualize on the first pass. Just read on the second pass. You should find that many of the images pop into your mind as you reread the list.

MALE NAMES (PART I)

Aaron—arrow
Adam—dam
Alan—land
Alex—all eggs
Andrew—ant drew
 Andy—dandy
 Drew—draw
Anthony—ant that's a ton
 Tony—toe

Arthur—otter
  Art—art
Barry—barrel
Brandon—branding
Brian—bright
Carl—curl
Carlos—car loose
Charles—charred
  Chuck—woodchuck
Christopher—crystal fur
  Chris—crystal
Dan—dam
Daniel—dam L
  Dan—dam
David—David and Goliath
  Dave—cave
Dennis—dentist
Donald—don a giant L
  Don—down
  Donny—don a giant E
Douglas—dig glass
  Doug—dig
Edward—head odd
  Ed—head
  Eddie—eddy
Eli—he lied
Emil—the mill
Eric—E on a rickshaw
Frank—frankfurter
Gary—carry
Gavin—gavel
George—gorge
Gregory—real gory
  Greg—great

Harold—hair old
  Harry—hairy
Henry—hen
  Hank—hank of hair
Howie—How?
Irving—nerve
Irwin—I win
Isadore—there's the door
Jacob—rake off
  Jake—rake
James—chains
  Jim—gym
Jason—J on the sun
Jay—a jay bird
Jeffrey—just free
Jeremy—chair me
Jerry—cherry
John—a john (bathroom)
  Jack—car jack
José—hose
Joseph—Sloppy Joe
  Joe—hoe
Joshua—jolly you are
  Josh—jostle
Juan—won
Jude—rude
Justin—just tin

If you've been through the list once, go back to the beginning and read it through again. If you've been through it twice . . .

Fix yourself a snack.

Something just occurred to me. You might be trying to do all your name training in one session. That's a possibility, of course, even if you've been taking your breaks. But it's probably not the best idea. You've spent most of your life without a trained memory. You can get by for one more day. Why don't you put the book aside and come back to it tomorrow? Just a thought.

When you're ready to push on, go through the next list and visualize, visualize, visualize.

MALE NAMES (PART II)
Keith—key
Kenneth—can in net
   Ken—can
Kevin—cavern
Kyle—wild
Larry—lair key
Larry—lariat
Lincoln—penny
Luis—wheeze
Manny—man
Mark—mark
Matthew—mat U
   Matt—mat
Michael—microphone L
   Mike—microphone

Nicholas—St. Nicholas
   Nick—nick
Nigel—night gel
Patrick—hat trick
   Pat—pat
Paul—pull
Peter—paid her
   Pete—pet
Ralph—growl
Raymond—ray mount
   Ray—ray
Richard—rich odd
   Rich—rich
   Rick—pick
Robert—robot
Roger—maharajah
Ronald—run old
   Ron—run
   Ronnie—running E
Ryan—rye in
Samuel—sand in the well
   Sam—sandwich
Scott—cot
Sean—yawn
Stephen—(see Steven)
Steven—stuff in
   Steve—leave
Ted—teddy bear
Thomas—tomcat S
   Tom—tomcat
Timothy—dim tea
   Tim—timber
Todd—toad
Victor—victory
Vincent—V on a cent

As I shake hands with "Sam Schuman," this is what might be going through my mind.

Walter—alter
Walt—wall
William—will M
Bill—dollar bill
Zachary—sack hill
Zack—sack

It's time for your final exercise—the last names. Read, visualize, and reread.

LAST NAMES
Abbott—I bought
Abel—a bell
Adams—dams
Alder—older
Alcott—all the cots

Allen—all in
Anderson—hand and son
Applegate—apple on a gate
Bailey—a bale of hay
Baker—baker
Baldwin—bald man winning (a race)
Brent—rent
Brown—brown bag
Calhoun—call home
Cameron—camera
Campbell—canned bell
Carter—cart
Clark—clerk
Collins—collar in
Cox—lox
Davis—Davis Cup
Drake—rake
Drew—draw
Eagan—eagle
Edwards—head words
Ellis—a wrist
Engle—angle
Evans—vans
Farber—far bar
Feldman—fell man
Garcia—car seat
Gibbons—ribbons
Gleason—grease on
Gonzalez—gondolas
Green—golf green
Hall—hall
Hammond—ham on
Harrington—herring that's a ton
Harris—hair is
Hernandez—her hand is
Hill—hill

Irving—nerve
Isaacs—eye sac
Jackson—Jack's son (Jack Frost, Jack be nimble,
    Jack Sprat)
Jaffe—coffee
Johnson—John's son (anyone named John)
Jonas—show us
Jones—owns
Kaplan—cap pin
Kelly—jelly
King—king
Lambert—lamb burr
Lee—lead (for a horse)
Lewis—loose
Lopez—low Pez container
Malone—a loan
Martin—martyr
Martinez—Marty's knees
McCoy—decoy
Mead—knead (bread)
Miller—miller (the occupation)
Mitchell—my shell
Moore—moor
Morris—more rice
Nash—ash
Nelson—melting son
Norris—nor us
Olsen—old son
O'Rourke—a roar
Palmer—palm
Parker—valet parker
Perez—pair of *S*'s
Philbin—fill the bin
Phillips—fill-ups (gas)
Quentin—quite a tin (can)
Rand—ran

Rhodes—road
Roberts—robots
Robinson—robin's son (baby bird)
Rodriguez—rod in a creek
Saunders—sander
Scott—cot
Seymour—see more
Smith—blacksmith
Tanner—sun tanner
Taub—daub
Taylor—tailor
Thomas—the mass
Thompson—Tom's son (tomcat, tom turkey, etc.)
Todd—toad
Turner—turner (acrobat)
Underman—under man
Ungar—hunger
Valdez—valley S
Vogel—vote & go
Walker—walker
Walsh—wash
Weber—web
White—white (ghost)
Williams—yams
Wilson—will and son
Wright—right hook (punch) or Wright brothers
York—New York
Young—young
Ziegler—zipper
Zucher—sicker

Here's what I might visualize the first time I meet "Beth Turner."

The term "absentminded" seems sometimes to suggest that the mind is altogether missing. In fact, it is often only absent from the practical tasks of everyday life, as in the case of the distinguished scientist, Sir Isaac Newton.

Newton was so preoccupied with his work that once he invited a guest to dinner, but failed to notice when the fellow arrived. The guest sat down quietly in the room and waited. When dinner was brought, there was only one plate of food, since Newton apparently had forgotten to inform the cook that he was expecting company.

Newton remained in meditation and ignored the food. After some time passed, his friend pulled up a chair to the table and ate the dinner. Not long after the man had finished, Newton came out of his reverie, looked at the empty plates on the table, and remarked, "If it weren't for the proof before my eyes, I could have sworn that I had not dined."

Perhaps the explanation for Newton's "absentmindedness" lies in his response to a question from an admirer, who once asked Sir Isaac how he had managed to make so many remarkable discoveries in astronomy. "By always thinking about them," he replied.

Apparently so.

FIVE

Face It

Oh, hi. You back? I was on the phone with a long-winded friend who's an avid "anecdote recycler." Well, as La Rochefoucauld once said, "Ain't it weird how folks can remember every detail of a story but they can't remember for the life of them that they've already told it to you a zillion times?" Or words to that effect.

You're ready for the final step now, the one that will make you Master of Names. You're going to hook your info-chain to one more image—a face. Obviously, the challenge here is not one of coming up with a visual translation of something verbal. A face is visual to begin with. And as we pointed out before, one of the amazing things about the human mind is the way it remembers faces. A computer might have to analyze a thousand or even ten thousand different aspects of a face in order to distinguish it from other faces. The human mind can see a face once for just an instant and then, for some reason we don't yet understand, recognize it again a month later. It doesn't matter that, in the meantime, the person who owns the mind has seen a few hundred other faces.

So you can remember the face. And now, thanks to info-chaining, you can remember the name. You know from experience that every info-chain has an open link on each end. But how do you attach that open link to the subtle, complex image of a human face? The answer is that you don't. You attach it to *one feature* of the face.

You've all seen caricatures of famous people. Jimmy Durante is all schnozz. Julia Roberts is all mouth. Telly Savalas is a chrome dome. The caricature artist looks at the face and chooses one or two distinctive features to exaggerate, making a simple sketch as instantly recognizable as a photograph. Look at the following caricatures and you'll see what I mean.

Fine, you say, but you're not a caricaturist. How do you pick out a feature? The way I do it is by scanning the face of the person I'm meeting. I call this "feature scanning." I do it the same way every time. I scan from left to right across the person's face at the level of the eyes. Then I cross back, diagonally and down, and then scan across at the level of the mouth and chin, making a Z pattern. The whole process takes only a few seconds. By the time I've finished my Zorro act, I've chosen a feature. With a little practice, you'll get to the point where you can do this quickly and easily, and then it will be like second nature to you. And don't worry, the other people will never know you're doing it. If they notice anything at all—and they won't—they'll simply be flattered that you're paying close attention to them.

In picking a feature, you have a lot of options to choose from—eyes, nose, lips, hair, eyebrows, eyelids, neck, hair color, glasses, chin, shape of face, cheeks, hairstyle, mustache, beard, even hat. To help you get the hang of this, I'm going to give you some photographs to work on. The first photo is of a friend of mine named Mr. Chester. Scan his face using the Z technique and choose a distinctive feature.

Mr. Chester

I'm going to tell you what feature I chose, but keep in mind that there's no right answer. Use whatever feature stands out to you. It's your brain and your memory we're working on here. I chose the eyebrows. They just struck me, probably because they're dark, in contrast to his light hair. You might have been struck by his full face or his pleasant smile or any number of things.

Okay, now I'm going to attach his name to his face. The image I came up with for Chester is a treasure chest. So I'm going to plop the chest right down on the eyebrows. In my brain's eye, of course. For an instant, as I'm being introduced to Mr. Chester, I will see a treasure chest sitting on his eyebrows. And the next time I see him, I will remember the name Chester. I *won't* necessarily remember the treasure chest. In fact, if Mr. Chester were wearing a hat or a cowboy scarf, you could choose that and it wouldn't matter if the next time you saw him he wasn't wearing it. You would still remember his name.

Forgive me if I repeat myself on that point. To me, that's one of the most interesting things about the way this system works. You can forget the mnemonic device and remember the fact. I have no objection to mnemonic devices that operate differently. "Thirty days hath September . . ." is useful in its own way. But I have to admit, those telephone numbers that match up to words drive me *crazy*. You know,1-800-USA-RAIL for Amtrak. I mean, it's great that you don't have to look up the number in the phone book, but it's a pain to have to hunt for those letters on the telephone keypad. Isn't it better to use a memory technique that helps you remember the number itself? (You'll learn this technique in chapter 9.)

All right, diversion finished. Let's get in a little more practice. We're going on to Ms. McLeod. Look at her face and choose a feature.

Ms. McLeod

Okay, I went with Ms. McLeod's ringlets. You could have chosen any other feature, but that's the one that struck me. Now I'm going to attach her name to the feature. I visualized McLeod as a cloud topped by McDonald's arches floating among the ringlets. It's that simple!

I'm not sure why this technique of attaching a name to one feature of a face works so well. Perhaps the simple act of choosing a feature focuses your attention on the face in a particularly helpful way. At any rate, it does work once you've practiced it a little. You'll probably feel self-conscious at first, but practice will help there, too. Just remind yourself of the rewards, the new confidence you'll have in business and social situations, and then go out there and do it.

Actually, to polish your skills in this particular technique, you don't have to go anywhere at all. I'm going to introduce you to a few more of my friends in the following pages.

Memory Exercise #10

Scan each face, select a feature, and then attach an image representing the name. Take your time at first. You can work on speed later. For now, you're simply working on understanding and mastering the technique.

If you're thinking right about now that this is not the easiest thing you've ever done, you're right. But trust me, this memory-building technique, like the other ones you'll find in this book, will get much easier with practice.

Ms. Nelson

Mr. Thompson

Ms. Gibbons

Mr. Crawford

Ms. Mercado

Ms. Barskaya

Mr. Quarles

Mr. Mandujano

Ms. Pankow

Ms. Rogalski

Possible Choices

Now I'm going to share the images I came up with for each of these people. If you had trouble with any of the faces, go back and review the picture after you've read my images for that person. That should help you get a better idea of how this works.

First there's Ms. Nelson. The feature I chose was her cheeks. You might have chosen her eyes or her light hair, but for me it was her cheeks. The image I used for Nelson was "melting sun." I saw the sun melting all over her cheeks. That was particularly easy because her whole expression is warm and sunny.

Next, there's Mr. Thompson. I was impressed by his smile. Then, to lock in his name, I pictured a tom turkey's son, a little turkey, running around the smile. He may not be smiling the next time I see him, but that won't make any difference! Once the association is made, the memory takes over and the original trigger isn't necessary.

It was Ms. Gibbons's eyes that struck me. I associated Gibbons with *ribbons* and pictured pastel ribbons fluttering all around her eyes.

Next we have Mr. Crawford. The young Mr. Crawford has a small, almost pug nose. I visualized a crawfish fording— wading across a stream running over his nose.

Our next friend is Ms. Mercado. When a face is as evenly featured as Ms. Mercado's, it can be difficult to single out a feature, but for some reason I chose her eyebrows, just as I did with Mr. Chester. Because my first language is English, I would go with the sounds in the name and choose the cue *Mercury*. Then I could imagine that her eyebrows were the wings of the winged messenger Mercury of Roman mythology. Alternately, I could have pictured a Mercury automobile cruising across her eyebrows. Now if my first language were Spanish, the name would be even easier, since *mercado* means "market." I could simply imagine a supermarket perched on those same dark eyebrows.

Then comes Ms. Barskaya. I chose her bangs as the face-link in the info-chain. For her name, I pictured a big candy bar in the sky, represented by a cloud. I see that candy bar set against Ms. Barskaya's bangs.

Let's see what we came up with for Mr. Quarles. I imagined a cartoon couple having "quarrels" on his nose.

What about Mr. Mandujano? His mustache is a convenient hook for an image. I decided to use *fondue* as my memory cue, so I dipped the end of Mr. Mandujano's mustache in a fondue pot.

What can we do with Ms. Pankow? The eyes have it for me. As for the name, this one is easy, isn't it? I imagined a cow sitting in a frying pan. So to link the name to the face, I see a cow in a frying pan floating past her eyes.

Finally, there's Ms. Rogalski. I was taken by her ears and imagined a rogue on skis, swooping down her ears.

Let me emphasize again that you're not going for elegance or perfection here, and you don't need to worry if the facial feature you chose was not the same as mine. It's all between you and your brain.

That's plenty of work for right now. Go take a short break and come back for the final flourish, when we connect the first names.

Stretch your legs

Refreshed and ready to go? Let's make chains.

In today's informal world, you will often be introduced to people by their first names. In that case, of course, you simply attach the first name to the facial image you've chosen. Most of the time, however, it's still important to remember the last name, especially in business situations.

If you have the last name in place, it's easy to add the first name. You just hook it up to the other links in the chain. Let's go to Mr. Chester, for example.

Mr. Chester's first name is Tony. You already have an image of a treasure chest sitting on his eyebrows. Now, what can we conjure up for the name Tony? You could go with a big toe. Then you could imagine a big toe poking out of the treasure chest. And don't worry about being disrespectful to old Tony. In the first place, he has a great sense of humor. In the second place, as I've said before, no one is going to read your mind in the few seconds it takes you to create your info-chain.

Now look at Ms. McLeod.

Ms. McLeod's first name is Liz. I simply added a lizard to the "McCloud" that is floating through her hair.

Now I'm going to give you the first names of our other friends so that you can practice your info-chaining.

Memory Exercise #11

Go back to look at each picture and try to add the first name to your memory info-chain. Remember, it can be attached to either the facial feature or the image of the last name.

JOYCE NELSON
FRANK THOMPSON
DEBORAH GIBBONS
DEX CRAWFORD

ESTELLA MERCADO
SHEILA BARSKAYA
DANIEL QUARLES
VICTOR MANDUJANO
EVA PANKOW
SARA ROGALSKI

How'd you do? Here's the way I approached these memory challenges.

Possible Choices

I stayed with a morning theme for Joyce Nelson. For Joyce, I used *juice*. I saw a glass of cold orange juice sitting on one of her cheeks as the sun melted all over them.

Frank Thompson's little tom turkey got a *frankfurter* to carry in his beak as he runs around Frank's mouth.

Deborah Gibbons's entire name seems to suggest feminine things to me. To remember her first name, I'll use *debutante*. I'll link the debutante to the ribbons by seeing her dressed in a white ball gown with the pastel ribbons swirling all over it.

Dex Crawford's crawfish now has a couple of *decks of cards* on his back as he fords the stream across Dex's nose.

If you happen to know that Estella means "star," you can add a star to Mercury's forehead or have a sale on stars at the supermarket. Otherwise, I would choose the image of a *cellar* and have Mercury running across Ms. Mercado's eyebrows and falling into a cellar.

For Sheila Barskaya I would add a large shield to that candy bar in the sky.

For Daniel Quarles we have a bit of serendipity. The cue I usually use for the name Daniel is "dam L." So of course I would place the quarreling couple on a beaver's *dam* on the bridge of his nose.

For the name Victor I like to use the idea of *victory*. How can I make that work with either the mustache on Mr. Mandujano's face or the fondue pot that I attached to the mustache? The key is to think absurdly. I'll see a boxer holding up his fist in the sign for victory, and he'll be standing in the fondue pot instead of a boxing ring.

Eva Pankow already has a cow in a frying pan floating past her eyes. I'm going to place *Eva Peron* on that cow, singing "Don't cry for me Argentina."

For Sara Rogalski, her rogue skier is now wearing a sari.

You've now learned the technique of matching names to faces. To lock in this new skill, practice is crucial. If you're not yet ready to face real people, you can use magazines. Any magazine contains dozens of pictures of people who are not celebrities. Their names will be unfamiliar to you. Practice on those names and faces.

You can also work on this technique while you're watching television. When a contestant is introduced on a game show, you have the perfect opportunity to scan the face and visualize the first and last name.

But first, take a break.

Take a short trip to dreamland.

Sometimes you have more to remember than just a name and a face. Sometimes there's a company name or a job title that you need to keep in mind as well. As you might guess, the thing to do in that case is add one more link to the chain. You've mastered chains of six or seven items and more. Four or five links should be no problem, with a little practice.

WHAT'S IN A FACE?

The main problem in face-recognition research is determining what attracts our attention. Do some features lend themselves to recognition better than others? In two recent experiments, hair was the feature quoted most often, followed by eyes, nose, face structure, and eyebrows (note these are all in the upper half of the face), then chin, lips, mouth, complexion, and cheeks. If this order indeed represents degrees of importance in recognition, then the Lone Ranger was really smart to wear a hat and a mask, thus hiding his hair, eyes, eyebrows, and most of his nose—four of the first five on the list. The last and presumably least important feature was the forehead, suggesting that trying to disguise yourself by wearing a headband is not a smart thing to do.

Jay Ingram, *The Science of Everyday Life*

Let's say that our friend Tony Chester is a sales rep for a printing company. Your chain already consists of a treasure chest sitting on Tony's eyebrows with a big toe sticking out of the chest. Now clamp a tiny printing press onto that big toe. If you want to highlight his position with the company, hang a "For Sale" sign on the press.

Joyce Nelson is the real estate agent who represents the couple who is buying your house. Joyce already has the sun melting on her cheeks and a glass of juice sitting on one of them. Now link your house to one of those images. Perhaps you could see your house perched on the rim of the glass, like a lemon slice. Now if you run into her at the grocery store, you'll remember her name and what she does for a living.

You can use this method to link any kind of information to a name and face. On the next page is a short list of occupations and businesses with some possible images for them. Use it as a guide to learn how to create memorable associations that work for you. Some of these associations are pretty obvious—a plunger for a plumber, for example. I mean, you'd hardly use a turnip, now would you?

Occupations

accountant	calculator
architect	blueprint
attorney	scales of justice
carpenter	hammer
clergy	praying hands
consultant	whispering in an ear
doctor	stethoscope
electrician	sparking wires
librarian	book
mechanic	wrench
plumber	plunger
printer	printing press
sales representative	"For Sale" sign
teacher	blackboard

Businesses

advertising	pitchman holding up container
appliances	washing machine
banking	safe
computers	keyboard
copies	two sheets of paper
hardware	screwdriver
hotel	bellman
house painting	dripping paint brush
office equipment	file cabinet
pest control	mouse
research and development	card catalog
stocks and bonds	stock certificate
travel agency	airline tickets

PART 2

Intense
Visualization

Here's Looking at You, Kid

Several decades ago, a computer expert named Von Neumann estimated that the human brain has, in computer terms, about 10^{20} bits of memory. That number looks like this:

100,000,000,000,000,000,000

Since then, dozens of other scientists have tried to estimate our capacity for memory based on such physiological aspects as the number of synapses in the average brain. Although most of the estimates have been somewhat smaller than Von Neumann's, they have been in the same ballpark—or order of magnitude, if you prefer.

Now another sort of scientist has approached the subject in a different way. Thomas K. Landauer, at Bell Communications Research, has run extensive tests to determine how much people can memorize in a given period of time. He concluded that human beings remember two bits per second "under all experimental conditions." Over the course of a lifetime, that would amount to about one billion bits of data. That number, 10^9, looks like this:

1,000,000,000

According to Landauer, then, humans don't have anywhere near as much memory as we once thought.

Well, they didn't test me. Nor did they test my students or any other memory trainers or "mentalists." And if that sounds egotistical, let me hasten to say that I'm just pointing out that they tested average, *twentieth-century* people with average, untrained, twentieth-century memories. These individuals had learned how to read and write early in life and therefore had never been particularly motivated to train their memories. If these scientists were trying to establish the human potential for memory, they might have tested some of us who've worked on developing and refining our skills. Otherwise, it's a lot like trying to determine the potential of the human body by testing a random sampling of couch potatoes instead of Jackie Joyner Kersee and Bruce Jenner.

Of course, there's another way to interpret Landauer's data. Look at those two numbers again.

100,000,000,000,000,000,000
1,000,000,000

What I see is a great many zeros' worth of unused potential. Is it possible that most people could remember 10 times as much? Or 100 times? Or more? The evidence is that not only *could* we, but that in the centuries before writing became common we *did*. In her landmark work, *The Art of Memory*, historian Frances Yates wrote:

> We moderns who have no memories at all may . . . employ from time to time some private mnemotechnic not of vital importance to us in our lives and professions. But in the ancient world, devoid of printing, without paper for note-taking or on which to type lectures, the trained memory was of vital importance. And the ancient memories were trained by an art which . . . could depend on faculties of intense visual memorization which we have lost (1966:).

Wow.
Back again, are you?

And just in time. I'm sure this Frances is some dame—
Yes, she is. A Dame of the British Empire, in fact. That's the female equivalent of being a knight, in case you're interested.

Whatever. Like I say, I'm sure she's the cat's pajamas, but what in the world is a mnemotechnic when it's at home?
That's just another word for a memory device.

And intense visualization?
I'm glad you asked that question.

Happy to be of help.
It's very simple, in principle. As we've seen again and again in this book, visual memory is very powerful. Associating two or more images has enabled us to remember names and faces with a fair degree of ease, and we've been able to string on any number of additional bits of information using our info-chain technique. The ability to see with the brain's eye has been of great value already. But what we've done so far is just the tip of the iceberg.

"Tip of the iceberg"? That's a pretty apt image itself!
It *is* apt. In Chapter 6, you'll find out just how powerful visualization can be.

Memory feeds imagination.

AMY TAN

Imagination feeds memory.

JON KEITH

SIX

The Brain's Eye

All right, everybody into the pool! Here's your first exercise.

Memory Exercise #12

Give yourself about a minute to look at the illustration below. Don't use your info-chaining techniques, but keep in mind that your memory will best retain what is meaningful.

Train good-bye

Now close your eyes and try to visualize the scene depicted in this illustration. Give yourself about a minute or so.

All right, now try to answer the following questions about the picture. If you have difficulty with any question, close your eyes and visualize the scene again.

Where is the scene located?
What is the couple on the right side of the scene doing?
Which person is leaning out the window?
Who is watching the couple?
What emotion is being expressed by the people watching?

Don't look back at the picture yet. If you're like most people, you were able to answer virtually every question. Now try this set.

What is the older man who's watching the couple holding
    in his hand?
Who can be seen just behind and to the left of the old man?
What is just above the small boy's head?
What is the older man wearing?
What kind of physique does the man in the couple have?
How many people in the picture are wearing hats?
Can you see the train's wheels?

Now you can look at the picture again. Did your visualization incorporate all these details? Did your brain's eye *fill in* the train's wheels? (That's one of the pitfalls of visual memory. It can sometimes join hands with imagination and play tricks on you.)

If you answered most of the questions in the second set correctly, your natural powers of visualization are quite good. No matter. The exercises that follow will help you improve your ability to construct, or reconstruct, images in your mind's eye. These exercises will also lay the foundation for some remarkably effective techniques based on memory methods that are centuries old. But I've updated the techniques to help you get the most from your memory in the twenty-first century.

Strength of mind is exercise, not rest.
ALEXANDER POPE

These visualization exercises have another benefit as well. They're wonderful "brain work" for keeping that organ active and healthy. A long-term, ongoing study of Alzheimer's disease patients and others suffering from forms of senile dementia has made it quite clear that "use it or lose it" applies to the mind as well as to the body. The subjects in this study belong to an order of nuns. In the controlled environment in which the sisters live, they all eat the same food, drink the same water, experience the same climatic conditions, and so forth. However, they are assigned different tasks and do different work. Over the decades-long course of this study, scientists have discovered that the nuns who have the most education and are most often engaged in mental work are the least likely to suffer from memory loss and other types of cognitive impairment. So these mental exercises will help you keep your memory fit, as well as improve your capacity for visualization.

All right, let's try another exercise.

Memory Exercise #13

Close your eyes. No, not yet! After you've read these directions. Close your eyes and visualize yourself walking through your front door. What's the first thing you see? Don't just say to yourself, "hall table" or "grandma's picture." Take a moment and really fix the object in your mind's eye. Then go on to the next picture or piece of furniture you see. In your mind, step into your living room and walk over to the sofa or your favorite chair. Sit down and try to visualize the room.

Scan each object and create a mental image, full of detail. Give yourself three or four minutes to do this exercise.

READY? START.

How'd you do? Did you have a sense of really seeing what was there? Did you see details you didn't expect to remember? If you're not in the living room already, go there and look at everything you see. What things did you miss when you were picturing the room in your mind's eye? Did you remember the painting over the television set? The silk flowers on the end table? Close your eyes again and fill in the gaps.

There are no right or wrong answers for this exercise. It's simply a workout for the mind's eye. Each time you practice the technique, you'll strengthen your capacity for visualization. Let's do one more visualization exercise before you take a break. This time I'm going to ask you to *add* to a picture in your mind.

Memory Exercise #14

Go back to the visualization of your living room. I want you to picture each of the ten items listed below and, in your mind's eye, place that item on an object in the room. You can use your sofa, a coffee table, the television set, a windowsill—any object you've already made part of your mental picture. Here are the items:

SWORD
TREE
RACCOON
MOTORBOAT
COVERED WAGON
PIGEON
CAMPFIRE
SUBMARINE

PILLAR
ACROBAT

Not your typical living room accessories, are they? As you go through the list, mentally walk through your living room, placing the objects one by one. When you've placed the last object, cover the page.

All right, now mentally walk through the room again, collecting the items. As you gather each one, write it down. Now uncover the page and compare your list to the one in the book.

How did you do? Were you able to "collect" everything you placed? For some people, this is an easier and faster method for remembering groups of things than info-chaining. The ancient Greeks built an entire memory system around it. For our purposes, it's the basis of a technique that can help you remember any set of related or unrelated bits of information. A medical student could use the technique to memorize the names of all the bones in the wrist. A marketing executive could use it to recall every point she wants to cover in a complex sales presentation.

We'll be working on this technique in chapter 7, right after you take a break.

Fix something around the house.

SEVEN

The Method of Loci

A Greek orator, Hotairius, stands in front of the Roman Senate, prepared to speak. He has a hard act to follow; Cicero just wowed 'em with some fancy verbal footwork. To make matters worse, there are rumors of a party over at Maximus's house, so the audience is getting restless. If Hotairius doesn't hold the crowd's attention, he'll lose them to cushions and peeled grapes. *And* it's half-price day at the baths. Not to mention the fact that PowerPoint hasn't been invented yet, so he doesn't have any slides.

This is a tough one. No stumbling, no rambling, no long pauses even. Thank goodness he has only 73 major points to make!

You think I'm kidding, right? Making a little memory joke? Not at all. According to the classical scholars, orators in the ancient world were able to speak about a topic for three and four hours at a stretch, without missing a beat, just by employing their powers of visualization. They stayed focused and built their argument step by step, using the Method of Loci (pronounced LO-key), a system invented by our old friend Simonides.

Loci is not some ancient oracle. It is simply the plural form of the word *locus*, which means "place." The Method of

Places. Essentially, the last exercise in chapter 6 employed a simplified version of this technique.

> The ostrich has a brain approximately the same size as its eye.

The ancient Greeks used a more complex method. The person who wanted to train his memory first visualized a physical location, such as his own home, in great detail. He physically walked through each room in the place and created detailed mental images of every scene. He noticed the peeling paint on a wall, the crack in a ceiling, even the way the light fell on a windowsill or a niche in the wall. After walking through the house physically, he walked through it mentally, recalling all those details and fixing them in his mind.

The next step was to choose the *loci*, the places in each room where the memory images could be set. Ordinary places, such as a chair or a shelf, were acceptable. Unusual places were even better, since the mind has a better recall of the unusual. The one absolute prerequisite was that each place be well lighted, so that the image would be clear.

Once the loci were chosen, they were never changed. They constituted the permanent memory framework for that individual, regardless of what he was trying to remember. Of course, the items placed at the loci changed with every task.

Hotairius, then, would have prepared for his speech by thinking it through as he made a mental walk through his house, placing images associated with the various points he wanted to make at the preestablished loci. Suppose, for example, he were presenting a budget. Some of the budget items might be road maintenance, viaduct building, military appropriations, bribes to foreign rulers, that sort of thing. He might choose images such as the following:

Topic	*Cue*	*Locus Point*
road maintenance	chariot	wall niche
viaduct building	waterfall	Venus de Milo
military appropriations	sword	hall windowsill
bribes	silver coins	bench

Our friend might begin his talk by picturing himself at the wall niche just inside the entrance to his home, where he would see a chariot. A few steps farther in, he would picture a waterfall gushing over his knock-off copy of the Venus de Milo. Making his way to a hallway windowsill, he would visualize a sword, shimmering in the sunlight. Then, as he turned the corner into his living room, he would imagine his low bench almost buried in silver coins. To make each image more memorable, he might add a vivid detail. For example, the chariot might have bright yellow wheels, or the sword might be coated with blood. The more striking the image, the easier it is to remember, as you know.

In any set of rooms, the ancient memory artist could find dozens, possibly even hundreds, of loci. However, some people went further and created their memory framework at a large public building. At the Acropolis, for example, the possibilities for loci were enormous.

In a nutshell, that's how the Method of Loci works. Now I'm going to give you a simple variation on it, sort of an update.

Memory Exercise #15

I refer to this as the Method of Choo-choo, which, you'll agree, is easier to pronounce than Loci. I want you to begin by visualizing a choo-choo train, the kind young children play with. Our choo-choo has six cars: a shiny black steam engine, followed by a coal car, a passenger car, a flat car, a box car, and a bright red caboose.

Got that? Engine, coal car, passenger car, flat car, box car, caboose. Close your eyes to help you fix the picture in your mind. All right, there's your memory framework.

Choo-choo train

Suppose you're driving home from work, thinking about the groceries you need to pick up at the supermarket on the way home. You can't stop the car to write down everything you need as you think of it. So you place the items, one by one, in each car of your train. Try it.

ZUCCHINI
MILK
PASTA
FRENCH BREAD
TOMATOES
WINE

All right, cover the page and see if you can remember the grocery list.

Cute, huh? You can remember any six items just like that. And the interesting thing is that you can use the train over and over. The next time you need it, just put your items into the cars and you've got it made.

Okay, we're going to move up to nine-item lists. For this, we're going to use a different framework. Ready?

Memory Exercise #16

Okay, now I want you to visualize a baseball diamond. The sun is blazing, the grass is a luxuriant green, and it's a beautiful day for a ball game. The pitcher is on the mound and the catcher is positioned behind the plate. Here are your baseball loci:

PITCHER
CATCHER
FIRST BASE
SECOND BASE
THIRD BASE
SHORTSTOP
LEFT FIELD
CENTER FIELD
RIGHT FIELD

Don't just look at the words. Put yourself in the scene. Get a mental picture of the baseball diamond, and imagine that you're at bat. You see the pitcher out there in front of you and the catcher behind you. Move your eyes around the bases, starting at first. Turn your attention to second base, then to third base, finishing your sweep of the infield at the shortstop position. Then gaze at the outfield, starting with the left fielder, going to center, and finally to the right field position.

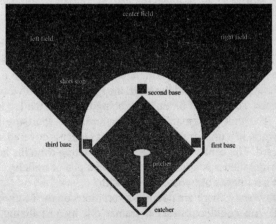

Baseball diamond

All right, here are the nine items you need to pick up at the mall.

At the office supply store:
STAPLER
FILE FOLDERS

At the supermarket:
DIAPERS
DOG FOOD
CHARCOAL
BRATWURST
MUSTARD

At the home and garden store:
SPRINKLER HEAD
MULCH

Locate each item on your imaginary baseball field. Exercise your creativity. Remember, you have the players to work with, as well as the field itself.

Possible Choices

This is what I came up with. I visualized the pitcher throwing a stapler instead of a ball. The catcher catches it in a file folder. As I look around the field, the first baseman is wearing a diaper. The second baseman is being bitten on the leg by a dog. The third baseman's hat is on fire. The shortstop is a bratwurst in a uniform and hat. The left fielder is covered with mustard. The center fielder has water spouting from his head. The right fielder is sitting unhappily on a pile of mulch.

What images did you come up with?

Obviously, there are countless variations on the Method of Loci. You could construct a framework by visualizing the members of your family gathered in some familiar location. Depending on how many relatives you include, you could have quite a number of loci. If you're an astronomy nut, you can make a ten-space framework using the nine planets and the asteroid belt. A cook might want to work with a spice rack. These systems are all fun and effective, and I encourage you to come up with memory frameworks of your own. The system has only one real drawback, besides the obvious limitations of size. The method helps you remember things in order, but it doesn't work so well if you want to recall, for example, the seventh item in a list. You usually have to count down to that item.

So I'm going to teach you a variation on the Method of Loci, one that works spectacularly well for me. Of course, first you have to take a break. Why don't you spend a few minutes visiting with a neighbor?

Pay a call on a neighbor.

EIGHT

Deep-Six Your Three-by-Fives

"I think I can, I think I can, I think I can."

What on earth is that?
The Little Engine That Could, of course. Didn't anyone ever read that book to you when you were a child?

Never mind that. Why are you doing a choo-choo cheer-leading chant?
I think it started way back in the middle of chapter 7, when I was explaining the Method of Choo-choo. Somehow, steam engines entered my train of thought, and since I kind of have a one-track mind I found myself engineering the conversation around to—

Stop, stop! If you have any pity, stop.
You certainly are sensitive. I was actually making a very important point, or reiterating it anyway.

Oh, yeah? What's that?
Simply that you can't approach this enterprise with a defeatist attitude. You have to be positive or you'll never get anywhere. If something looks difficult, try it anyway. Then at least you can say it's difficult with some authority.

Seriously, I've done thousands of seminars and taught these skills to tens of thousands of people, and I can say with certainty that they're *not that hard* to learn. They are skills, and they require a little practice, but nothing we're working on is as challenging as, say, learning to play golf or perfecting a tennis serve. They're not even as difficult as beginner's bridge.

If it helps you, draw symbols and images when you're doing associations. Some people find it much easier to remember things when they draw or diagram. Others need to hear or say things out loud. Experiment until you find your prime learning style and everything in this book will go more smoothly. I promise.

So think like the Little Engine That Could and move along with me to a dandy little memory framework I like to call the "idea catchers." It's a bit more sophisticated than the frameworks we used in chapter 7, primarily because it allows you to remember things in and out of order. With the idea catchers, you can instantly recall the third or seventh or ninth item in a list, without having to run through the entire sequence.

All right, we're going to begin with what I call "Jon Keith's Five-Foot Shelf." Just visualize a shelf attached to a wall and on it place the following objects:

> AN ARROW POINTING STRAIGHT UP
> A SWAN
> A THREE-LEAF CLOVER
> A BANNER
> A CUP HOOK
> AN OLD-FASHIONED BOMB
> A FIDDLER
> A SNOWMAN
> A LONG-TAILED CAT
> AN EGG

These are your Idea Catchers. They represent—and look like—the numbers 1 through 10. You can use them over and over, whenever you want to remember things that are ranked. They should look something like this:

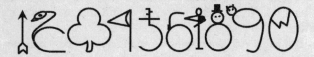

Actually, this drawing is only to give you an idea of why I chose these images. When you visualize the objects in your mind, fill in any details you'd like. Your swan can be a magnificent, snowy-white creature, floating on a deep blue lagoon. Or perhaps you're thinking of a mighty blackbird with her great wings extended, ready for battle. Your fiddler can be an Appalachian bluegrass musician or Itzhak Perlman. I doubt that you can do much with the cup hook, but give it your best shot.

Now take a few minutes to visualize each of these images in your own way before we go on. When you're finished adding more details to your idea catchers, I'll ask you to do one last thing.

Have you made each image vivid enough to remember? Great. Now get rid of the shelf. That's right, we don't need it anymore. With the idea catchers, you don't need loci. You're going to attach images for the things you need to remember directly to the idea catchers. Are you ready? Let's try it out.

Memory Exercise #17

The American Film Institute recently released a list of the 50 greatest female film stars. Using the idea catchers, you should be able to memorize the top ten names on this list in a matter of minutes. If you're really familiar with these actresses, you can link their faces to the idea catchers. If these women are unfamiliar to you, come up with images for their last names and link those to the idea catchers. Either way, have some fun with this one.

1. KATHARINE HEPBURN
2. BETTE DAVIS
3. AUDREY HEPBURN
4. INGRID BERGMAN
5. GRETA GARBO
6. MARILYN MONROE
7. ELIZABETH TAYLOR
8. JUDY GARLAND
9. MARLENE DIETRICH
10. JOAN CRAWFORD

Possible Choices

How did it go for you?

For number 1, I visualized Katharine Hepburn riding an arrow straight to a bull's-eye, just as she always did in her movies (in my humble opinion).

For number 2, I saw Bette Davis sitting astride a swan, surveying the lake around her and saying haughtily, "What a dump!"

For 3, I imagined Audrey Hepburn as Holly Golightly in *Breakfast at Tiffany's*, dressed in the height of fashion, holding a long cigarette holder, and perched elegantly on a three-leaf clover that curved around her like a beanbag chair.

For 4, I visualized Ingrid Bergman in Rick's Café, holding a banner that said "Play it again, Sam."

For number 5, I imagined Greta Garbo in a coffee cup dangling from the cup hook. Leaning over toward the cup, I could hear her murmur, "I *vant* to be alone."

For number 6, I saw Marilyn Monroe tossing a water bomb into an audience, giggling her trademark giggle.

For 7, I imagined Elizabeth Taylor in her famous movie

role as Cleopatra, stretched out next to Nero, who fiddled while Rome burned.

For 8, I saw Judy Garland on the yellow brick road with an extra friend. Alongside the scarecrow, the tin man, and the lion, there was a snowman.

For 9, I saw Marlene Dietrich as a cat in a top hat, singing "Falling in Love Again" onstage in a smoky cabaret.

Finally, for 10, I visualized an egg done up in Joan Crawford's trademark shoulder pads and heavy eyebrows.

All right, just in case you're not a film buff, I'll give you another list.

Memory Exercise #18

These are the kinds of wedding anniversary gifts you're supposed to give to mark the first ten years of marriage. Use the idea catchers to commit the list to memory.

1. COTTON
2. PAPER
3. LEATHER
4. FRUIT AND FLOWERS
5. WOOD
6. SUGAR
7. WOOL
8. BRONZE
9. POTTERY
10. TIN

Possible Choices

Year 1—I visualized an arrow landing in a huge mound of fluffy white cotton.

Year 2—I imagined a flock of origami swans flying over an origami mountain.

Year 3—I saw a leprechaun in a black leather motorcycle jacket decorated with a clover insignia.

Year 4—I pictured various kinds of fruits and flowers marching in a parade, carrying banners.

Year 5—I imagined a sculptor carving away at an enormous wooden cup hook.

Year 6—I visualized a cake decorated with half a dozen miniature bombs made of sugar.

Year 7—I saw a mountain fiddler surrounded by sheep whose wool had just been shaved off.

Year 8—I imagined a snowman striking a big bronze gong.

Year 9—I saw dozens of cats climbing up the side of a huge pottery jar, trying to get to the milk inside.

Year 10—I visualized a hen sitting on a nest of tin cans in place of the usual eggs.

Take a break now. When you get back, I'm going to explain what this framework is useful for, besides filling your head with cocktail party conversation

Have some fun with your family.

Right. Onward and upward. You should be pretty familiar with the idea catchers by now, but you may be wondering about their usefulness. I can answer that in one word—speeches. It doesn't matter whether you're giving one or listening to one; this framework is ideal for helping you remember the major points of any presentation.

Let's suppose you're a sales representative and you're going to be introducing a new, redesigned reclining chair to an important client who's considering buying several hundred of these chairs for some model homes. You have a lot of material to cover, and it's the first time you're making this presentation, but you don't want to use notes. I suggest you write out your key points and then attach each one to an idea catcher. I'll go through the exercise with you to show you how it's done.

Presentation Points
1. We value your business.
2. New recliner has revolutionary design for maximum versatility.
3. The name of the new model is the "Emperor."
4. Sturdier construction.
5. Expanded selection of upholstery fabrics.
6. Two-speed vibrating feature.
7. Available for a limited time at an introductory wholesale price.
8. Speedier delivery from the factory.
9. New cleaning service.
10. Best warranty in the furniture industry.

Matching Each Point to an Idea Catcher
1. I would visualize something that represents the buyer's business, such as a bill of sale. I would then use an arrow to attach a blue ribbon to the bill of sale.
2. I see a bunch of swans marching with big signs that read "Revolution Now!"

3. I imagine a three-leaf clover walking along wearing a big crown.
4. I see a construction site with banners flying all around it.
5. I visualize dozens of fabric swatches attached to a very large cup hook.
6. I see a bomb shaking slowly, then fast.
7. I imagine a fiddler with money falling from his pockets and stuffed into his boots and hat.
8. I see a snowman on skates speeding across a pond.
9. I imagine using a cat as a dust mop. (Just kidding!)
10. I see a warranty with a fried egg affixed to it instead of a seal.

Now let's see if you can do one.

Memory Exercise #19

You've been asked to talk to your garden club about growing flowers from seed. Here are the ten major points you'd like to cover:

Presentation Points
1. Choose seeds matched to your climate.
2. Seeds should suit your sunlight conditions.
3. Plant at the proper time of year.
4. Use a "grow light" if you're starting your flowers inside.
5. Use a good potting-soil mix.
6. Plant seeds at the appropriate depth.
7. Water from below to encourage root growth.
8. As soon as the weather begins to get warmer, take plants outside a few hours each day to make them hardy.
9. Transplant seedlings with great care.
10. Water frequently for the first week or two.

Possible choices

1. I visualized an arrow shivering in a cold rain.
2. I saw a swan pulling the sun across the sky.
3. I imagined a calendar page decorated with clovers.
4. I saw a banner waving in the air with a blinding light behind it.
5. I pictured a cartoonlike cup hook trying to dig its way out of a mound of dirt.
6. I visualized a bomb dropped into a hole in the ground.
7. I saw a fiddler pouring water from a violin.
8. I imagined a snowman beginning to melt in the sun.
9. I pictured a cat walking very carefully along a fence.
10. I saw a watering can pouring out a stream of eggs.

You probably noticed that there were a number of similar points in the garden-club speech. That's not a problem with the idea catchers because they provide you with an exact sequence, so you won't mistake one point for another.

Of course, you can also use the idea catchers to focus your memory when you're listening to a speech. When you hear an important point you'd like to recall later, just link it to an idea catcher. When the talk is over, you'll have an outline that will help you remember the entire presentation in proper sequence.

Obviously, you can create more idea catchers for longer speeches. However, later in the book, I'm going to be introducing another memory framework with a virtually unlimited capacity.

For now, why don't you try these ten idea catchers on a few more lists? It's good practice, and you'll be able to amaze your friends with your knowledge. Well, maybe not *amaze*. More like mildly surprise. But when was the last time you did that?

Do I need to remind you to take a break before you try these? I didn't think so. Just have some fun with them any time you want to, but for now . . .

Invent something.

Practice Lists

THE HIGHEST MOUNTAINS IN THE UNITED STATES
1. McKinley (Denali)
2. St. Elias
3. Foraker
4. Bona
5. Blackburn
6. Kennedy
7. Sanford
8. South Buttress
9. Vancouver
10. Churchill

THE COUNTRIES WITH THE MOST ELEPHANTS
1. Zaire
2. Tanzania
3. Gabon
4. Congo
5. Botswana
6. Zimbabwe
7. Zambia

8. Sudan
9. Kenya
10. Cameroon

THE WORLD'S LARGEST CARNIVORES
1. Southern elephant seal
2. Walrus
3. Steller sea lion
4. Grizzly bear
5. Polar bear
6. Tiger
7. Lion
8. American black bear
9. Giant panda
10. Spectacled bear

THE MOST COMMON NAMES FOR POPES
1. John
2. Gregory
3. Benedict
4. Clement
5. Innocent *and* Leo (tie)
7. Pius
8. Boniface
9. Alexander *and* Urban (tie)

PART 3

The Number/Sound System

A World Filled with Numbers

Once upon a time there was a nice little company that manufactured quidgets. In this company, the benevolent president loved his employees, and workers didn't want to work anywhere else. The pay was fair and the benefits were good. The president shook hands with the night watchman and asked about his children and grandchildren. When an employee celebrated a birthday, there was cake with candles in the cafeteria. It was a nice little company.

The years passed, and then one day the quidgets this company manufactured were found to be absolutely vital for making top-secret blodgets, a key component essential to the high-stakes aerospace industry.

Overnight, it seemed, the quidget company doubled, then quintupled in size. The factory went high-tech and moved to a new security-conscious facility. The kindly president was replaced by a tough-thinking, bottom-line CEO, the night watchman by a building-wide security system, and birthday cake by a computer-generated note on a pay stub reading "Hoppy Birthday." (The computer didn't have a spell checker.) Every employee was screened for a top-security clearance and issued a 9-digit identification number, which he or she had to enter on keypads at the factory gate, at the factory door, at the turnstile that led to the work floor, and even at the door to the employee bathroom. The company had entered the electronic age.

One day, George Wilson, a loyal employee for thirty years, left for work but showed up back on his own doorstep at 9:30 in the morning. He handed his wife his lunch pail and hung up his jacket.

"What's wrong, George?" cried Mrs. Wilson. "Are you ill? Are the quidget-cutters on strike? Did you get fired?"

"Worse," he replied glumly, sinking into his recliner and reaching for the remote. "My goose is cooked. It's all over. I can never go back there again. I forgot my employee identification number."

That was a terrible joke.
It wasn't a joke at all. It was an illustrative story.

Then it was a terrible illustrative story. What was the moral? That some people are too dumb to live?
I was trying to make the point, as vividly as possible, that today's world is filled with numbers. And that anyone who wants to function in that world had better have a good memory for digits.

Oh, come on. There aren't that many numbers.
Well, there are student identification numbers, personal identification numbers, driver's license numbers, and social security numbers. There are phone-card numbers and discount long-distance numbers. The average business phone number, with area code and extension, is at least thirteen digits long. You have a savings account number, a checking account number, and a number to call when you need to check on your checking account.

Okay, I get the point.
There are stock quotes and computer codes, appointment dates and meeting times. You have—

I said I got the point. But can't I just write everything down in my appointment book?
Not a good idea. In the first place, some of these numbers should never be written down anywhere at any time, for security reasons. Others should not be written down in anything so easily lost or stolen as an appointment book. And others you just need to remember for a few minutes at a time. They'd clutter up your appointment book in a New York minute.

Isn't that better than cluttering up my mind?
That's one of the lovely things about minds. They don't clutter as easily as you might think. And, of course, we're going to use the four skills—association, visualization, imagination, and organization—to keep things under control.

Most people can remember seven digits for a minute or two, until their attention is distracted. It's particularly easy if you "chunk" the number by dividing it into more manageable bits: 2754409 is more formidable than 275-4409.

There are some easy ways to remember short numbers, particularly if you need to remember them only briefly. Probably all of us remember a few phone numbers by the pattern they make on the telephone keypad. I never forget my friend Jack's phone number because the last four digits fall at the outer corners of the keypad: 1397. My aunt Helen has a number that's a snap to remember, because her phone exchange is the same as mine and the last four digits begin with zero and then take a jog to the right and go straight up the keypad: 0963. So, you see, figuring out keypad patterns can be a handy memory aid in some cases.

What if I don't have a keypad handy?
There are other patterns that work just as well. Some numbers fall into place arithmetically, particularly if you have a good feel for math. Take the phone number 765-7050, for example. Notice that the first three numbers are a countdown from 7, and the last four numbers repeat the first and third, with zeros

between them. By the time you've finished working out the pattern in a number, you'll probably remember that number for life.

And if I don't have a flair for math?

Well, a history buff might remember some numbers by associating them with past events. No matter where these turn up, remembering them would be a snap: 1492, 1066, 1776, 1864, 1941. The rest of us, on the other hand, might have to use mnemonic devices to remember those historic dates in the first place. You know, "In fourteen hundred and ninety-two, Columbus sailed the ocean blue."

In any case, the most effective method for remembering numbers is one that can handle any number at any time. As we know by now, the mind puts information away so neatly and quickly that it can often never be found again—unless you've attached a tag to it. That, of course, is what we've been doing throughout this book. It's also what we're about to do with numbers. We're going to tag all these numbers with images so you can pull them out of the file, one two three.

Hold on. I understand about making images out of words. But how do you propose to make an image out of a number?

It's easier than you might think. Watch and learn.

 Take the Pressure Off Your Memory

Here's an easy way to eliminate one memory frustration—remembering where you've put all those small things you use often but can never find: keys, scissors, pen, adhesive tape, stamps, glue stick, and so on. Stash everything in a basket you keep by the phone.

NINE

The World Is So Full of a Number of Things

Ready to jump right in? Great. Make this word into a number.

MOSQUITO

How'd you do? If you're a numerologist, you took the alphabetical ranking of each number, added its digits to get a single digit, then added that number to those of all the other letters and came up with 39, which you could then reduce to 12 and finally to 3. None of which would do you any good here. Or if you're the touchy-feely type, maybe you simply *felt* that the word *mosquito* had a sort of 643 quality to it. Or maybe you thought, "The old boy has lost it now," and simply skipped the whole thing.

Well, you're about to discover that, in mnemonic terms, "mosquito" is 3071. And that fact will prove to be the key to remembering numbers.

If you've been using the techniques you've learned so far in this book, you understand how easy it is to remember information that is associated with a visual image. Logically, then, we should find a way to associate a visual image with any number that you need to remember. Fortunately for us, memory experts have been doing that very thing for a long time. In fact, the first system for "spelling numbers" was developed in the early 1700s by an English clergyman named Richard Grey. It was refined over the years and, in the 1840s, an American named Pliny Miles created the three-step system that virtually all memory trainers use today.

Step One: Assign a consonant sound to each digit of a multidigit number. Miles and his predecessors put the consonants into ten linguistic sound groups and assigned each group to a digit. Ten sounds, ten digits.

Step Two: Throw in all the vowels you want to connect to the consonant sounds. That is, turn the consonants into a word.

Step Three: Visualize the word and remember it.

At first this technique may seem a little complicated and contrived, but work through the exercise with me and I think you'll find it's actually simple and effective. The key is to connect the ten digits with ten sounds. Once you have that part down, everything else follows.

I've had people in my classes who initially declared that the number/sound system would "never work," but then surprised themselves by reciting multidigit numbers backwards and forwards by the end of one class period.

I'll never forget Gus, a sales representative who came into a seminar looking as though he had a gun under his jacket. It was his booklet of style numbers, account numbers, order numbers, and so forth. He resisted the number/sound system ferociously, saying that he could always write things down, he had his own system to remember numbers, all the usual excuses. I finally talked him into giving the system a try, since he was going to be spending time in the seminar anyway.

A couple of months later, Gus got in touch with me again. He had used the system to memorize all those numbers and pretty soon he had a reputation in the company for being really on top of things. That led to a promotion, and Gus was now sales manager. It was a big payoff for a relatively small investment in time and energy.

Of course, if you have no reason to remember long numbers in your business or social life, you can just skip this section of the book. But I'd recommend you give it a try. Even if you decide not to take it any further after reading the material, you will have improved your memory for numbers just because you will see them in a different way.

All right, are you ready to start? I'm going to give you the sounds that Miles assigned to each digit. Don't try to commit them to memory yet. We'll take care of that later.

1	2	3	4	5	6	7	8	9	0
T	N	M	R	L	J	K	F	P	S
D					Sh	C(hard)	V	B	C(soft)
					Ch	G(hard)			Z
					G(soft)	Q			

Now don't be put off by the fact that some of the numbers are related to more than one letter. Basically, you have to remember only the first letter in each group. The others make exactly the same sound or are phonetically very close. If you say them out loud, you'll hear the similarity. Your mouth and tongue do almost exactly the same things when you say *T* and *D*. Pronounce *utter* and *udder* and you'll see what I mean. The same is true for other groupings. Say *Jerry, Cherry,* and *Sherry.* Notice how your mouth kind of puckers up and you push air through your teeth? Of course, *K, Q,* and hard *C* represent the same sound—ask anyone who owns a Kountry Kitchen or a Kwicker Printer—and hard *G* is very close. Say *tricker* and *trigger.* As for *F* and *V,* most of us say "I hafta" instead of "I have to." That's how close those two sounds are. These sound groupings are ones that lip readers find almost impossible to distinguish.

You may have noticed that we're dealing only with consonants here. The vowels—*A,E,I,O,U*—and near vowels—*Y,W,* and *H*—are utterly irrelevant in this system. So is the *G* that comes after *N* in words like *sing* and *sang*. That *G* doesn't behave like a nice, normal consonant, and we won't be bothered with it. We'll use these letters as spackle to hold our words together, but that's their only purpose in this system.

> **Memory is the cabinet of imagination, the treasury of reason. . . .**
>
> **SAINT BASIL**

Now that you know how the system works, I'm going to give you a set of memory cues to help you memorize the number/sound combinations. Of course, different memory trainers have used different cues over the centuries. I've designed the following cues to appeal to associations you may already have with individual numbers and to reinforce the sounds through alliteration.

Of course, you can come up with your own cues if you like, now that you're so good at associations. The important thing is to remember the number/sound combinations. Once you have committed these ten combinations to memory, they will help you remember any number you ever encounter in the future. I think you'll find, as Gus did, that it's a small investment of time and effort for a large payoff.

All right, here's my set of memory cues. Read through the cues once, visualizing as you go.

1 = T (also D)	Visualize 1 lonely golf tee on the first hole.
2 = N	Visualize 2 twin nuns named Nan and Ann.
3 = M	Visualize the 3M logo or 3 massive mountains.

4 = R	Visualize 4 right turns bringing you right back where you *are* to begin with.
5 = L	Visualize the 5 sections of a maple leaf.
6 = J (also soft G, Sh, and Ch)	Visualize 6 jet engines, three on each wing of a jet airplane.
7 = K (also hard C and hard G)	Visualize 7 kings from 7 countries on the 7 continents.
8 = F (also V)	Visualize a skater gliding over the ice in a figure 8.
9 = P (also B)	Visualize Pluto, the 9th planet in our solar system.
0 = S (also Z and soft C)	Visualize a sailor sending an SOS.

By this time, if you've done your visualizations correctly, you probably know most of the pairs. So cover the page and try to write them from memory. Don't worry about the secondary letters. Just write the primary letter associated with each number. After you've done that, look at the list again. Review the pairs you had forgotten and then cover the page again. Try once again to write the pairs. Then go on to the exercise.

If you don't know all the pairs now, by the time you finish the next couple of exercises they will be thoroughly fixed in your mind. You should also use the 1-2-5 method, going over the list once more at the end of your work today, once tomorrow, and once again in five days.

On the other hand, if you're just reading about this technique without doing the work, you may be thinking that this is really, really *hard*. It might even be as difficult as, say, learning the ranking of hands in poker. Well, just remember that there were a lot of illiterate cowboys in the Old West who knew that a straight flush beats a full house.

I guarantee that if you're even slightly motivated, you can learn the number/sound system just as easily. If you're not motivated, that's another story. Just move ahead to Part IV of the book.

One final note. Keep in mind that we're interested only in the *sounds* of the letters. If the consonants are silent in a particular word, forget them. *Light* has two consonant sounds—L and T. *Rough* has two consonant sounds—R and F. In each word, the G is silent. Also, if a letter appears more than once but makes only one sound, it counts only once. *Kipper* has only three consonant sounds—K, P, and R—even though it has four consonants.

Still wondering why *mosquito* is 3071? Here's the explanation. We begin with the number, because that's what we're trying to remember. Let's say it's my friend Stewart's apartment number in a high-rise building. I visit old Stew every month or so, and each time I have to ask the lady at the desk to ring his apartment because I've forgotten the number. Or I could do this:

M S K T
3 0 7 1

Once you have the consonants set in sequence, you get to play. You add vowels of your choice and come up with *musket* or *mesquite* or *mosquito*. I liked mosquito, so that's what I went with. Now I just think about a mosquito biting my pal Stew and make a beeline for the 30th floor and apartment 3071.

Just to make sure you have the idea, I'm going to translate a couple of other numbers. Let's do another four-digit sequence, a PIN number. This time, it's 1548.

T L R F
1 5 4 8

I think I'll go with "tile roof" here. Then I'll lock it in by visualizing a tile roof on my ATM machine.

Or what about the zip code for my friend Kathleen? It's 98575, and my first try at conversion gives me this:

P F L K L
9 8 5 7 5

Nothing leaps to mind for me with this letter sequence, so I'm going to try the alternate members of some of the letter groups.

B F L G L
9 8 5 7 5

What I see now is "baffle gull." As luck would have it, Kathleen lives not far from the ocean and she's a little eccentric, so it's very easy for me to imagine her walking along the beach confusing a seagull. Even if she lived in the desert, however, I could use the image.

I suspect it's time for a five-minute break now. Why don't you give your mind a rest and get some exercise?

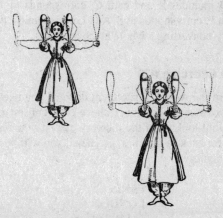

Get some exercise.

Back? Good. Just for practice, I'm going to give you words and phrases that I created from various numbers and see if you can convert them back into the numbers. That will give you a feeling for the kinds of words you might come up with. Later we'll do it the other way around. Remember to concentrate on the consonant sounds only. Begin with this one.

PULL

The answer here is 95. P corresponds to 9, and L corresponds to 5. Now try another.

STAIR

The number here is 014. Zero matches up with S, Z and soft C. T, like D, goes with 1. And R is 4.

Here's another word.

GAVEL

You should have come up with 785. Hard G, part of the group that includes K and hard C, corresponds to 7. The V, along with F, corresponds to 8. And L corresponds to 5.

Now try converting a whole batch of words.

Memory Exercise #20

Here are the words. Write them down if you need to, and put the corresponding number above each consonant sound. Do it without looking at the memory cues if you can. If you need to refer back to the cues, go ahead. You will be reinforcing your memory.

PARIS
LONDON
JAMMING

TOP PEG
MITTEN
FAMILIES
LUCKY ME

Answers

Here's what you should have come up with.

PARIS	940
LONDON	5212
JAMMING	632
TOP PEG	1997
MITTEN	312
FAMILIES	8350
LUCKY ME	573

I'm sure you did a splendid job. I just want to point out a couple of places where you might have gone astray. In the third example—*jamming*—you might have come up with two 3s because there are two *M*s in *jamming*. This could happen only if you forgot that we are dealing only with sounds. There is just one *M* sound in the word *jamming*, even though there are two *M*s, so there is only one 3 in the number. Then again, you might have matched a number to the *G* at the end of the word. But it's neither a soft nor a hard *G*, so you probably remembered that for the purpose of this exercise, it doesn't exist. We don't give a hang about the *G* that comes after *N*.

Memory is a capricious and arbitrary creature. You never can tell what pebble she will pick up from the shore of life to keep among her treasures.

HENRY VAN DYKE

When I converted 1997 to words, I needed two separate *P* sounds, which forced me to use two words. I don't know of any word in the English language with a double *P* and two different *P* sounds. I don't even know how that would work.

So apart from the double letters and double numbers, this system is pretty straightforward. One consonant sound per number, all the vowel sounds you want, and you've got it!

If you've been working along with me, by this point you probably have the number/sound combinations pretty much down pat. From now on, try to do the exercises entirely "from memory."

This time, I'll give you the numbers and *you* come up with the words. After all, that's the way it works when you're trying to recall a number. Here's the catch: I don't want you to write anything down. I want you to do this work in your head. Don't worry, the numbers won't be very long, and I'm going to give you some practice first.

All right. Just relax. Look at the number and let the consonant sounds pop into your mind one by one. Then use those consonants to create a word. Start with this one.

091

Okay. The consonants are SPT. You could have come up with *spit* or *spot*. The number 1 can also correspond to D, of course, so you might have come up with *spud, speed,* or *sipped.* If you used one of the optional consonants for 1 and 9, you might have come up with *zipped, sobbed,* or any one of dozens of others. The thing to remember is that those options are available if you need them. But if you can make a word out of the first letters that pop into your head when you see a number, that's perfectly fine.

Now try this one. Concentrate on the number. Close your eyes if you like and see it with your brain's eye.

The consonants are NST. You might have come up with *nest* or *nasty*. For this combination of consonants, I can't think of dozens of other words. I'm stuck with a nasty old nest.

One more example. Rid your mind of distractions and concentrate. Replace the digits with letters and hear the sounds.

432

The consonants are RMN. You could use those letters to come up with *rooming, roaming*, or even *Roman*.

Memory Exercise #21

Now try your skills on this list. Focus. Replace. Hear the sounds.

185
645
231
642
746
351

Possible Choices

Here's what I came up with. For 185, I got *the file*, the biggest nail file in the world. For 645, the word I came up with was the name *Sheryl*. For 231, I decided on *nomad*. When I looked at 642, that "share" sound came to mind again, along with an N this time, so I went with *sharing*.

You'll find that after you have some practice with this technique, certain number combinations instantly suggest words or word parts like that. The conversion process will become automatic and therefore much easier.

I converted the number 746 into *crush*. And for 351 I came up with *melt*.

I think that's about it for this session. Time for a break.

Hold on a minute. I know that some of you are tempted to go back and look at the list of memory cues, aren't you? Don't do it, okay? You can review them after your break. At the moment, your brain wants nothing to do with them. I'm not saying that you'd short-circuit your synapses or anything like that. It's just that after a period of intense concentration, you sometimes reach a point of diminishing returns. If you're so absorbed in the learning process that you can't think of anything else to do, here's a suggestion:

Fix yourself some dinner.

Benjamin Disraeli, prime minister of England in the second half of the nineteenth century, once ran into someone whose name he had forgotten. Quite embarrassed, Disraeli stalled for a moment, then rescued himself with a question that suggested he remembered the man quite well: "And how is the old complaint?"

In 1981, the London *Times* offered a similar question, perfect for those literary cocktail parties we all attend: "How's the book?"

These days, the appropriate all-purpose question seems to be, "Are things any better at work?"

TEN

Life Is Just a Bowl of Numbers

Let's dive in with a refresher and then we'll talk. Convert these numbers into words.

$$620$$
$$914$$
$$751$$
$$195$$
$$414$$

Here's what I came up with.

SHINS
BUTTER
KILT
TABLE
RUDDER

Hmm. It's a list of words. Suddenly, I have this over-whelming desire to do something with this list of words. What could it be? What do I *usually* do with a list of words? I've got it! I'll info-chain it.

I see a pair of scrawny, hairy shins and someone is slathering butter on them. Then I see dozens of sticks of butter put together to make a kilt. I see a kilt being used as a curtain around a vanity table. Then I see a table with a rudder sailing across a lake.

By George, I've just memorized the 15-digit number 620,914,751,195,414.

Neat trick, huh? Of course, even if you did all the steps along with me, that 15-digit number didn't just pop into your head at the end. For someone who has practiced this number/sound system, it works very much that way, though. The info-chain fades away and the number remains. You'll begin experiencing that phenomenon as we work on this technique, but it does take a while. Be patient and you'll be rewarded.

You can recognize the principle at work here. Once you convert numbers into words, you can convert the words into images. Once you have your images, you can make info-chains. That means you can remember extremely long numbers as easily as you now remember a grocery list. (I'm assuming that you've put your memory work into practice and can remember your grocery list with ease.)

> **God gave us memory so that we might have roses in December.**
>
> **J. M. BARRIE**

Knowing the principle is only the first step, however. Learning these techniques is a process. You're training your brain, not just informing it. So it's crucial to go slowly and build each step on the one before. If you get impatient and rush the process, you'll fail and you'll think the system has failed.

Of course, different people learn at different rates, but you should notice a change in the way your mind registers numbers immediately. If you *never* apply the system, your memory for numbers will still be improved.

After the first day, if you do the exercises, you will be able to memorize multidigit numbers backwards and forwards, even if you have to check your list of number/sounds occasionally. Your progress after that will depend on how much you apply the system, but people who use it all the time, every day, have been known to master it in a week or two.

That's why this book is written the way it is. I want your reading experience to be as close as possible to what you might experience in one of my memory courses. There's explanation, practice, reinforcement, humor, encouragement— all the things it takes to make improved memory a part of your life. If you just work with me, you'll end up with a sharper memory that will benefit you every day. Other people will react to you differently, and you will feel better about yourself. But you need to follow the steps and do each one of the—

Yeah, yeah, yeah.
What? What are you doing here?

You were preaching.
I was *not* preaching. This just happens to be an important point and I wanted to make sure I got it across.

You were preaching. You do that, you know.
Well . . . training memories is what I do. It's important to me. I've seen how it gives people confidence and makes their lives easier.

I've taught memory techniques to a lot of senior citizens who had started to believe what society is always saying about older people—that their minds begin to go and they can't remember things. They would say things like, "Oh, this stuff will work when you're with me, but it's really you doing it."

After awhile, though, they begin applying the techniques in

their lives and it renews their self-confidence. It's a great thing to see. I want everyone to experience that boost in self-esteem. And I know that just reading this book won't do it. You have to make memory enhancement an active learning experience, doing each and every exercise. This number/sound system is especially useful, but it does take some time and effort to master. You need to do the work in order to get the benefit.

But not every reader will be so engaged. Face it. For some people, this is just an interesting book, not a commitment. I know you're right. It's just that it really takes so little effort to make such gains, and when you think about the tremendous—

Most of them will learn something, Jon. Sure. Sure they will. A simple association technique. A memory shortcut or two. That's nothing to sneeze at. If they just pay more attention to things, focus a little more, that alone will improve their memories say, five or ten percent.

That's right. Buck up, old man. The readers who really want to learn this are counting on you. And they're getting tired of me. Of course. Sorry. Let me just pull myself together.

PAUSE WHILE JON PULLS HIMSELF TOGETHER.

Okay, I'm fine. Now, let's do just one more set of three-digit numbers.

Memory Exercise #22

Let your mind relax. If it helps you, close your eyes after you look at a number so that nothing distracts you. Replace the digits with consonant sounds. Say them out loud—the sounds, not the letters. Go.

461
839
262
754
728
218
415

Possible Choices

461 = rigid (image: someone rigid with fright, unable to
    move)
839 = vamp (image: Theda Bara or Madonna)
262 = nation (image: map of the U.S.)
754 = killer (image: killer bee)
728 = can of (image: tin can of whatever)
218 = native (image: Native American)
415 = riddle (image: someone looking puzzled)

Obviously, this gets easier as it goes along, but I can't
spend the whole book giving you number lists. Besides,
they're pretty easy to come up with on your own. I strongly
suggest that you practice on whatever numbers come your
way. Street addresses. Phone numbers. Dates. Try writing
down the birthdays of all your children and/or nieces and
nephews and/or brothers and sisters. Use numbers for the
months as well as days. July 14 would be 714, or kiter. (That's
a person who flies a kite.)

If you're feeling up to it, we're going to go on to four-digit
numbers.

Memory Exercise #23

Transform these numbers into words, and then fix each
word in your mind with an image—the more ridiculous, the
better. In some cases, you'll be able to do the job in just one

word. In others, you'll go to two words. You may split the sounds into 3 and 1, 2 and 2, or 1 and 3—whatever works for you.

> 2161
>
> 4482
>
> 4013
>
> 6130
>
> 3867
>
> 9950

Possible Choices

How did you do? Here's what I came up with.

2161 = not shut (image: an open door)

4482 = rare fan (image: an exquisitely painted fan)

4013 = roast 'em (image: a barbeque grill and a plate of hot dogs)

6130 = jet homes (image: a bunch of mobile homes with jet engines)

3867 = move shake (image: a soda jerk tossing a milk shake back and forth)

9950 = bubbles (image: a million bubbles in the sky)

You now have a lot to work with and a lot to work on. You should not go on to the next chapter today. What I suggest is that you take a break and then practice the number/sound system for the rest of the day as you go about your business (or tomorrow, if you're reading this at night). Convert every set of two-, three-, and four-digit numbers you see.

If you go grocery shopping, convert the prices. Just push your cart through the aisles and think to yourself, "Carrots, 59 cents a bunch—59, LP, *lap*. Bunch of carrots in my lap. Avocado, $1.38—138, TMF, *time off*. Take time off to eat an avocado. Cookies, $2.98—298, NBF, *no beef* in these cookies." When you get to the checkout, watch the scanner to see how many of the numbers you can remember correctly.

One caution. Take care not to run down small children with your cart while you're practicing this technique. It's easy to do if you're concentrating, and children are more important than number sounds.

You can, of course, also practice in a hardware store, a clothing store, or an outlet mall. It may even help keep you within your budget. Just vow not to buy anything that requires an info-chain of more than two images.

Another place that's ripe for number picking is the library. Convert the call numbers as you browse. At a restaurant, convert the prices on the menu. If you're staying at home, flip through your telephone book, a gold mine of numbers. Or glance over your child's shoulder while he's doing his math homework and mutter "unicorn," "gas," "petticoat."

Or maybe not. You can take this thing too far. For example, you should *not* try to memorize license plates while you're driving, or you'll miss your exit on the highway.

At any rate, go now. There's a world of numbers out there, just waiting to be memorized

---

Life goes by, trivial things happen to us, important things happen to us. Now, it would make a lot of sense, wouldn't it, because we have a brain that probably has some limited capacity of some kind . . . to have a brain which stored to a more intense extent those things that are important and to a lesser extent those things that are trivial? We *have* a brain that does that. And it's emotions that create a relationship between the importance of an event and how well we remember that event.

—Neurobiologist James McGaugh, *a specialist in the physiological basis of memory*

ELEVEN

One for the Money, Two for the Show

I have a friend. We'll call her Agnes. Agnes will not buy a combination lock because she always forgets combinations. At the health club, she has to exercise with a key on a string around her neck so that she can get into her locker afterwards. She keeps the key to her storage locker on a nail in her kitchen because she already has too many keys on her key chain. Of course, every time she goes to the locker, she ends up having to return home because she's forgotten to take the key. Agnes's life is a comedy of keys because she is so afraid of combinations.

And yet, what is the average combination? Three numbers of one or two digits. An incredibly simple info-chain. And so, in honor of Agnes, I'd like to begin this chapter with a few padlock combinations. Convert the numbers to consonant sounds, create words and images, and then info-chain.

The one difference here is that I want you to add one image to the beginning of the chain. That image will tell you what the number is for. For example, if the combination is for your health-club locker, you might begin with a stair machine. In fact, we'll do exactly that.

Are you watching, Agnes?

health club locker: 31-21-9

The sound equivalents for this combination are *mt, nt,* and *p.* Here are the words I used—*mutt, nut,* and *up.* I began by imagining a stair machine, to indicate a health club, and I put a big old mutt on it, with his paws on the handlebars. Then I saw a huge peanut, with the mutt lounging on it like a deck chair. The final image in the chain is an acorn zooming up into an oak tree, like a movie running backwards.

To demonstrate how flexible this system is, here's another solution for the same combination. If I use *md* instead of *mt* and *nd* instead of *nt,* I might come up with the words *maid, nod,* and *pie.* I could visualize a maid on the stair machine, dusting as she exercises. Then I might see a maid with a nodding head, like one of those little bobbling toys you put in the window of a car. Finally, I might imagine a pie nodding off to sleep.

All right, the next combination is for a bicycle lock.

bicycle lock: 25-6-18

The sound equivalents here are *nl, sh,* and *tf.* The words I used were *nail, shoe,* and *tough.* I began with a bicycle running over a bed of nails. Then I saw a huge shoe trying to hammer a nail. Finally, I imagined the shoe dressed like a tough guy, in a black leather jacket, with a cigarette hanging out of its mouth.

I could just as easily have used *nl, j,* and *df.* Then my words might have been *nail, jay,* and *daffy*. I'll let you work out the images.

Okay, now for the padlock on a box of important papers.

important papers box: 14-20-32

The sound equivalents of 14, 20, and 32 are *dr, ns,* and *mn,* and the words these sounds triggered for me were *deer, noise,* and *man*. My first image was that of a last will and testament being read after a funeral to a room full of weeping deer dressed in black. Then I imagined the world's only clumsy deer running through the forest making an incredible amount of noise. Finally, a loud noise scares a man half to death.

Of course, the same sound equivalents can yield different words. For example, 14 could be *tr,* and even though 20 remains *ns,* and 32 remains *mn,* you could come up with the words *tree, nose,* and *moan*. Again, I'll leave the images up to you.

One more and then we'll go on. Might as well do the storage locker. Save Agnes an extra trip.

storage locker: 34-17-10

The sound equivalents are *mr, tg,* and *ts*. The words I came up with for this one were *mare, tag,* and *toss*. To match the storage locker, I'm picturing a supersize storage box. Inside it, a mare is trying hard to make herself comfortable. I then link this image to one of a meadow in which several mares are playing tag. For the final link in the chain I see a couple of big luggage tags tossing a ball back and forth. Ridiculous? Absolutely. That's why it works.

Alternatively, you might have used any of the following groups of words—*Mary, tack,* and *toes; homer, tug,* and *dice; mire, duck,* and *daisy*. The freedom to choose any letters within the designated sound group gives you a lot of options.

With any luck, we've just cured Agnes of her fear of combinations. You've also had a little more practice with the number/sound technique. By the way, how'd it go at the grocery store? Did you do some covert converting? Well, if you didn't, there's always today.

Actually, this might be a good time to remind you that it's really fun to practice this particular skill with a partner. You and your partner can work back and forth, converting numbers to info-chains and back again. As you get better at it, reduce the time you give yourself to do each set. Challenging yourself this way will speed up the learning process and make practicing a lot more entertaining.

Just a little test, now. What's the health club combination?

Did you remember it? I'm betting that you did. Probably you had to recall the info-chain and then decode it. But it won't be long before the numbers pop right up and the images you used to lock them into your memory vanish.

You've now mastered six-digit numbers. Didn't even notice that, did you? Well, the obvious place to go from here is to the world's most dreaded seven-digit number combination—the phone number. If you can info-chain six numbers, you can do seven. Again, we're going to attach the number to something relevant—the person's name. We'll begin with Ms. Gleiter in shipping. Ready?

Gleiter 625-3954

How did it feel doing your first telephone number? You can't really complain. You got more than halfway through the book before I made you do it.

I'll tell you what I came up with for this one. I saw a glider for the name. The consonant equivalents for the numbers are *chnl* and *mblr*, and the words I used were *channel* and *ambler*. So my info-chain was a glider soaring over the English Channel, then a TV channel on which all the people were amblers (people walking aimlessly). Of course, if I wanted to get really complicated, I could picture an ambler walking over a shipping bill. Then I'd also remember what department Ms. Gleiter worked in. But that's just a little frill. We'll stick with the basics. Next name and number, please.

Marshall 402-6320

The name suggested an image immediately, of course—a Western marshal with a shiny star. By matching the numbers to consonant sounds, I came up with *rsn* and *chmns*, so I chose the words *raisin* and *chimneys*. So I'm imagining a marshal in a shoot-out with an enormous raisin. Then I'm seeing raisins spewing from a bunch of chimneys instead of smoke. Let's do another.

Clifton 275-0619

Well, that one didn't fall into place quite as easily for me, but I managed something. For the name, I went with *cliff*. The sound equivalents were *nkl* and *sshtp*, and out of those letters I created the words *nickel* and *sash tip*. You know, the tip of a fabric sash. I know it's not an elegant solution, but that's completely unimportant. If it works, it works. To sum it up, I see a huge nickel rolling off the side of a cliff. Then I see a tiny nickel hanging from the sash tip.

How's your brain feeling? It's not the end of the chapter yet, but I think it's time for a break.

Close your eyes and think heavenly thoughts.

Okay, we've just done seven digits and we're not going to stop there. We're going on to some style numbers on dresses your boss wants you to pull out of stock for her.

So you don't have a boss and you haul bags in a feed store. Just work with me, all right?

The dresses you're looking for are the black ruffled one, style number 130-382-984; the red sequined one, style number 692-159-740; the white lace one, style number 954-964-153; and the turquoise leather one, style number 272-485-113. You can't just go by the description, because there are several red sequined dresses, dozens of white lace ones, and even three black ruffled ones. There's only one dress in turquoise leather, but you're just lucky on that one. One at a time, now. Go for it.

black ruffles: 130-382-984

What did you come up with? I started with those black ruffles, a ready-made image. The numbers matched up to the sounds *dms, mvn,* and *bfr,* so I used the words *dimes, moving,* and *buffer.* For my images, I hung hundreds of bright silver dimes from the ruffles. Then I visualized a family of dimes on moving day. Finally, I imagined a buffer moving across a floor by itself. Next.

red sequins: 692-159-740

With the red sequins fixed in my mind, I matched the number combinations to *shpn*, *tlp*, and *grs* and came up with the words *shipping*, *tulip*, and *grass*. For my first image, I wrote a shipping bill on an oversized red sequin. Then I pictured a tulip garden in which the petals were made of shipping tags. Finally I saw a bunch of tiny tulips with tall grass growing between the stems.

white lace: 954-964-153

I started by picturing a huge mound of white lace. Using the number/sound technique I came up with *plr*, *pgr*, and *dlm*, which, to me, suggested the words *pillar*, *pager*, and *deal 'em*. First I imagined a mound of white lace as tall as a pillar. Then I saw a little pillar beeping like a pager. Next I visualized a pager sitting at a poker table snarling "Deal 'em!"

Okay, just one more example and we'll relax and tell jokes.

turquoise leather: 272-485-113

The sound equivalents are *nkn*, *rfl*, and *ttm*, so the words I came up with for this one were *nick in*, *raffle*, and *totem*. I started off by imagining a wall of turquoise leather with a nick in it. Then I pictured St. Nick in the tumbling basket at a raffle, and then I saw Raffles—the gentleman burglar—climbing a totem pole.

Ready for a breather? Okay, I told you we'd tell jokes.

I was talking to my friend Jennie the other day. I asked her if she was still taking her ginkgo. "When I remember," she replied.

Stand-up comic Paula Poundstone got it in a nutshell

when she said, "I have short-term memory loss, though I like to think of it as presidential eligibility."

And now, if you want more jokes, go turn on the television. It's time for another break.

Take a ride.

Back refreshed and ready? You'd better be. We're going to tackle the big ones. Loooooong numbers. Really looooooong numbers. But don't worry. You'll have no trouble at all.

If you've been doing the work all along.

And *if* you took a break.

The fact is, you've already done NINE-digit numbers. Those are pretty impressive memory challenges. And, as you've seen, the great thing about long numbers is that you can break them up into groups of short numbers. For instance, if I give you

575920658876

you're not going to be intimidated. You'll immediately break the number up into

575-920-658-876

and get to work. Just make the number/sound conversions and then info-chain. "Chain, chain, chaiiiiiiin. Chain of images." (Forgive me, Aretha.)

575-920-658-876
lcl-bns-shlf-vcsh

Here's what I got. I converted 575-920-658-876 into the words *alcohol, bones, shelf,* and *heavy cash.* First I saw bones instead of a container of alcohol in my medicine cabinet. Then I got a mental picture of many bones on a closet shelf. Finally I visualized a shelf about to break under the weight of a heavy pile of cash.

Of course, you don't always have to use groups of three. If the sounds fall more naturally into other groupings, that's fine. For beginners, though, it's probably best to start with threes.

Okay, here's another one. Go ahead, make your chain.

794835217098

This one turned out a little strange for me. Well, that happens sometimes, and I just go with it. I came up with *keeper, female newt, kiss,* and *puff.* Honestly. Well, look at the sounds!

kprfmlntkspf

In my info-chain I have a zookeeper trying to catch a female newt, which I picture as a lizard with long eyelashes. Then I see that female newt kissing her powder puff. Clear as the nose on your face. All right, one more for good luck.

7357469510141

Let's look at the sounds again, just for the heck of it.

kmlkrjpltstrt

By now, I'm hoping that when you see a *K*, you immediately think of hard *C* and hard *G* as well, and that a *J* is just shorthand for *J, Sh,* and *Ch. T* can just as easily be *D*, and so forth. The sound/number options are second nature to me by now, so I came up with *camel, groucho, pole, daisy, hatter,* and *tea.* This makes for another memorable info-chain: A camel is being ridden by Groucho Marx. Then Groucho is climbing up a very tall pole. The pole has a huge daisy blossom at the top. Then I see daisies strung around the Mad Hatter's hat. And the Mad Hatter is, of course, sipping tea.

Once you've mastered this basic technique, there's really no limit to the number of digits you can handle. Just remember how you get to Carnegie Hall:

Practice, practice, practice.

TWELVE

From Here to Eternity (Almost)

Before we move on to memorizing passwords, the bane of our existence at the dawn of the twenty-first century, here's an entire chapter of number challenges for you to practice on. I'm sure I don't have to remind you not to work through the entire chapter in one sitting. The rule is fifteen minutes of work, then a five-minute break. If you have a timer, it's a good idea to set it for your practice session. Have a little discipline. If you work for too long at one stretch, you won't learn as well. The work will also get harder, and you'll get frustrated. You'll sit there thinking about the sounds *C* and *T* and not be able to come up with a single image for them. (Here, kitty, kitty.)

When you're working on the short numbers, try to do them in your head, without writing anything down. Someday you'll do that with the longer numbers as well, but not just yet. If any of the practice exercises trip you up, you'll find some possible choices at the end of the chapter, beginning on page 137.

Good luck.

Practice Exercise #1

DOUBLE DIGITS
   10
   39
   07
   65
   98
   79

Practice Exercise #2

THREE DIGITS
   123
   474
   147
   195
   914
   857
   200

Practice Exercise #3

FOUR, FIVE, AND SIX DIGITS
   4695
   3624
   3194
   92267
   76749
   74564
   201426
   074912
   492514

Practice Exercise #4

PHONE NUMBERS
424-8802
732-6985
571-0348
645-8164
354-7120

Practice Exercise #5

LOOOOOONG NUMBERS
94741297004
190265125649
557494380282

Possible Choices

PRACTICE EXERCISE #1: Double Digits

Possible Choices
1 0
toes

3 9
mop

0 7
sock

6 5
jelly

9 8
beef

7 9
gap

PRACTICE EXERCISE #2: Three Digits

Possible Choices

1 2 3
denim

4 7 4
rocker

1 4 7
truck

1 9 5
table

9 1 4
battery

8 5 7
flag

2 0 0
noses

PRACTICE EXERCISE #3: Four, Five, and Six Digits

Possible Choices

4 6 9 5
rch bl
roach bell
Info-chain: a giant roach ringing a bell
or
rg pl
Reggie pill
Info-chain: Reggie Jackson throwing a pill instead of a ball

3 6 2 4
mchnr
machinery
Info-chain: a silly machine

or
msh nr
mush narrow
Info-chain: a very long, narrow bowl of mush

3 1 9 4
mitt bear
Info-chain: a baseball mitt on a bear

9 2 2 6 7
banana shake
Info-chain: a giant banana shake

7 6 7 4 9
cash crop
Info-chain: a crop of cash growing in a field

7 4 5 6 4
gorilla chair
Info-chain: a gorilla sitting in a chair

2 0 1 4 2 6
nest orange
Info-chain: a nest of oranges

0 7 4 9 1 2
cigar button
Info-chain: a cigar buttoning its vest

4 9 2 5 1 4
robin ladder
Info-chain: a robin climbing a ladder

PRACTICE EXERCISE #4: Phone Numbers

Possible Choices
424-8802
rnr-fvsn
runner five song
Info-chain: a runner doing a 5K race while singing a song

732-6985
kmn-shpfl
key man shipful
Info-chain: a whole shipful of key men (locksmiths)

571-0348
lkt-smrf
locket Smurf
Info-chain: a locket containing a smiling picture of a Smurf

645-8164
jrl-ftjr
jar left jar
Info-chain: a drill sergeant yelling, "Jar, left, Jar" to a group of soldiers marching in formation with jars on their feet

354-7120
mlr-ktns
mailer kittens
Info-chain: a padded mailer envelope stuffed with kittens

PRACTICE EXERCISE #5: Loooooong Numbers

Possible Choices

94-7412-97-004
br grdn bk ssr
bear garden book saucer
Info-chain: A large grizzly bear is working in a little garden path. There is a garden in which nothing is growing except books. A book is floating through the sky like a flying saucer.

190-265-125-649
tps njl tnl shrb
tapes angel tunnel shrub
Info-chain: Your audio tapes are being played by an angel. (It could happen!) An angel is flying through a tunnel. Shrubs are driving into a tunnel instead of cars.

557-494-380-282
llc rbr mvs n fn
lilac rubber movies no fan
Info-chain: The smell of lilacs is rising from the rubber
gloves you are wearing. Rubber gloves are acting in
movies instead of people. You go to the movies to get cool
because it is sweltering and you have no fan.

A clarinetist once approached the great conductor Toscanini
and said apologetically that he would be unable to play that
evening because the E-natural key on his clarinet was broken.
Toscanini thought for a moment and then said, "It's all right.
You don't have an E-natural tonight."

THIRTEEN

Passwords

A decade ago, who would have thought that forgetting passwords would become one of the biggest headaches in American business? A password used to be something you gave to the guard at the gate of a military encampment or the name of a television quiz show hosted by Alan Ludden. Today, significant dollars in productivity are lost every year because beleaguered corporate employees can't recall one or more of the dozen passwords they're expected to keep locked in their brains. Supervisors find top-secret passwords pasted under computer desks or scrawled on file folders, because the pressure to remember is simply too great.

One computer systems administrator keeps a folder of passwords under lock and key in a separate location so that he can rescue the employees who come to him wringing their hands. Each password is listed under the three initials of the employee who is using it. One distraught worker came to him after a week's vacation, having forgotten the master password that would give her access to all her work files. When the administrator looked it up, he thought he was seeing double. The password *was* her initials! Now that's someone with a memory problem!

Usually, however, the problem with remembering passwords is that security demands you choose something *un-memorable* in order to make it unguessable. If you use a password drawn from your own life—your birthday or your dog's name—it will usually be easy for you to remember. It's a built-in trigger for your memory. But if anyone is really determined to violate your security, he or she can find out your dog's name without much trouble.

So, you might ask, can't you just go with a cue word that's a little more obscure, perhaps a name from the past, someone you can remember but no one else will know? Possibly. Say you have to come up with a password that your computer will ask for every time you turn it on. Choosing one obscure but memorable name from a lifetime of acquaintances may not be too difficult. There's always the first boy you ever kissed or the girl you took to the prom. As long as you didn't marry that person, it might be a fairly good choice, not easily guessed.

But suppose you're in a security-conscious office and you're required to *change* your password every month? You could have a problem coming up with enough words that are highly memorable to you and unknown to anyone else—not to mention the challenge of remembering which password you're using this month.

And that's not the only issue. Your password must be not only un*guess*able, but un*crack*able. There are computer hackers who specialize in cracking passwords, just as there are people who crack safes. To protect yourself from that kind of security violation, your password is going to have to be pretty sophisticated.

The following list of requirements for a good password was put together by a security specialist. First, the don'ts:

1. Don't use your login name in any form (as-is, reversed, capitalized, doubled, etc.).
2. Don't use your first or last name in any form.

3. Don't use your spouse's name or your child's name.
4. Don't use other information easily obtained about you. This includes birthdate, license plate number, telephone number, Social Security number, the brand of your automobile, the name of the street you live on, and so forth.
5. Don't use an all-number password, or all the same letter. This significantly decreases the search time for a hacker.
6. Don't use a word contained in (English or foreign language) dictionaries, spelling lists, or other lists of words.
7. Don't use a password shorter than six characters.

Now, the dos:

1. *Do* use a password with mixed-case alphabetics—that is, a combination of upper and lower case characters.
2. *Do* use a password with nonalphabetic characters—for example, digits or punctuation.
3. *Do* use a password that is easy to remember, so you don't have to write it down. (Italics mine.)

Don't you love it? After nine rules that encourage you to make it really difficult to remember your password, you have a tenth rule that tells you to make it easy to remember. Well, it can be done.

As you might guess, the number/sound system is excellent for passwords. It allows you to handle any password assigned to you, and you can also use it to create passwords that are easy for you to remember but impossible for anyone else to guess.

Suppose you're looking for an eight-digit password. You choose any eight digits at random. Throw a pair of dice. Hit the numbers on a pocket calculator with your eyes closed. Open a book to several different pages and string the numbers together. Here's a password number I came up with by rolling dice:

75734888

When I transform the digits to sounds, I get

KLKMRFFF

That converts easily to *clock, morph*, and *fife*. What I visualize is an old-fashioned alarm clock morphing into Barney Fife. When I recall that image, I'll remember the password number easily, and it's so random that I'm confident that no one else in the world could crack it.

But our expert—and most others—suggests that the most secure passwords are those that contain a combination of numbers and letters. But mixing letters into the regular number/sound sequence can lead to chaos.

So I'm going to give you a list of simple images that correspond to the letters of the alphabet, specifically to use with passwords and other letter-number combinations. You probably won't use them for any other purpose, but they're excellent for creating links in your info-chains. The images are based on the *sounds* of the letters of the alphabet, so read them aloud and, as usual, conjure the images in your brain's eye.

In some cases, I've modified images that have been used by memory trainers for centuries. Others have stood the test of time. All are easy to remember.

A	ape
B	bee
C	sea
D	dean
E	eel
F	fork
G	G-man (federal agent type)
H	H-bomb (a mushroom cloud)
I	eye
J	jaybird (use your imagination)
K	cake

L	elevated railroad
M	ember (as in a fire)
N	inn
O	Oh! (an exclamation point)
P	pea
Q	cue stick (for playing pool)
R	hour (a clock)
S	Eskimo
T	tea (bag)
U	U-boat (submarine)
V	V-neck (sweater)
W	water
X	X-ray (machine)
Y	why? (a question mark)
Z	zebra

Now I want you to read through the list again, just once. Don't waste your time reading the list over and over. You'll learn the images best by using them in the exercises. To help lock the images into memory, review the list tomorrow and then again five days from now.

When you combine the alphabet pictures with number/sound info-chains, you can handle any password your company dishes out, and you can construct passwords that would baffle any cryptographer. You'll be able to take any random grouping of letters and numbers and make it meaningful enough for you to remember. Take this password, for example:

6BX23A

To create an info-chain, you could start with *shoe*, use *bee* and *X-ray* for the letters, then move on to *enemy*, and use *ape* for the final letter. I link it all together this way: In my mind I picture a big old shoe on a small bee. Then a very large bee is getting an X-ray. Next, I'm doing an X-ray of my enemy. In the final image, my enemy is an ape.

As with any other info-chain, this group of images will not stay with you forever. The images behind the numbers and letters will fade, and you'll simply remember the password. If you don't believe me, try it. Just use the info-chain once tomorrow to help you remember it. Then review the password five days from now. It will be there. Let's do another one.

971H64DF

My info-chain links for this one would be *pocket, H-bomb, jar, dean, fork.* I visualize a shirt pocket with a mushroom cloud rising out of it. Then I see a mushroom cloud coming out of a jar. Finally, I imagine a jar sitting in the dean's office waiting to be reprimanded with a fork.

Okay, time to practice. Here are some passwords to convert and memorize.

Memory Exercise #24

Convert each of the following passwords into an info-chain.

53M3898KD
TR54I62
976AZ
30QZ854

Possible Choices

Here are the info-chains I came up with:

53M3898KD—lamb, ember, muff, puff, cake, dean
I visualize a lamb warming itself at a huge glowing ember. An ember causes a furry black muff to burst into flames. A furry black muff is used as a powder puff. A powder puff sits

down to eat a whole birthday cake. A cake beams with joy when it sees its name on the dean's list.

TR54I62—*tea, hour, Larry, eye, shine*

I imagine that a large tea bag is the pendulum in a grandfather clock. A clock is sitting on top of my friend Larry. Larry is pushing a large glass eye up a hill. An eye shines like a beacon.

976AZ—*package, ape, zebra*

I see a package being carried by an ape riding a zebra with a package under his arm.

30QZ854—*moose, cue stick, zebra, flower*

I see a moose playing pool with a cue stick. Then I imagine a bunch of cue sticks as stripes on a zebra. Finally, I see a zebra sitting under a tree smelling a flower.

That's one way to approach the password issue. Here's another. If you're asked to create your own password, choose a long word at random from the dictionary and convert it to letter sounds. Here's one I chose:

ridiculousness

In numbers, this word becomes 4175020. Now you don't want to jot down the word to help you remember the numbers. Believe it or not, there are a lot of people out there who know the number/sound system.

It's smarter to come up with an image that will keep the word in your mind. For example, you could imagine a bunch of clowns behaving in all kinds of ridiculous ways. Or you could see a guy who's always the "life of the party" wearing a lampshade on his head and singing *Danny Boy*.

Here are some practice exercises that give you a chance to try out your new skill.

Memory Exercise #25

Just to see how far you've come, try converting these into passwords as quickly as you can and without looking back at our original list of number/sound equivalents.

constituency
magnificence
electroencephalogram
antidisestablishmentarianism

ANSWERS
7201120
3728020
57142085743
2110019563214203

Up to now, the methods we've been working on have all been based on the number/sound system. However, if you're more comfortable with the Method of Loci, you can apply that to passwords just as easily. Simply create your password from random words that can be attached to images, and then position those images in your brain's-eye view of your home or office. Further ensure the security of your password by randomly capitalizing letters or adding symbols. Let's try one.

I'm going to choose two words that have no meaning for me. For security's sake, I will deliberately *not* choose a word associated with anything within view of my computer. And since I seem to favor animals when I make up my word lists, I'll also stay away from animals. I think I'll go with *gear* and *hinge*, capitalize both the *G*'s, and add a 7 at the end.

GearhinGe7

All right, these are the steps I will take to place my images.

1. In my brain's eye, the first thing I see as I enter my office is a low bookcase. I'm going to imagine an old, rusty gear on top of that bookcase.

2. The next thing I see is a potted plant, so I'm going to picture that plant with a hinge in its stem, allowing it to be bent in half.

3. The third locus I'm going to use is an armchair I keep for visitors. I'll picture one of the seven dwarfs sitting in that armchair.

4. Finally, under the armchair, I'm going to visualize a pile of capital *G*'s so that I will remember to capitalize the *G*'s in the password.

Since it seems that we're all called upon to create and use passwords more and more these days, before we move off the subject, I'd like to pass along a few more tips recommended by security experts. Use the memory techniques you've learned here to help you remember any password you create.

1. *Choose a line or two from a song or poem and create your password by using the first letter of each word.* You can use association and/or info-chaining to remember the song or poem you've selected. For example, if you chose "I'm forever blowing bubbles, pretty bubbles in the air," your password would be ifbbpbita. You might then capitalize the *b*'s for additional security, though many systems no longer require a case sensitive password. To remember the song, you could visualize a bee busily trying to burst a spray of bubbles.

2. *Choose two short words and put them together with some punctuation in between.* Make an info-chain out of the words and the punctuation. Suppose you chose *ocean* and *lock* and linked them with an exclamation point. You could visualize an ocean wave sweeping over a huge exclamation point, then imagine an exclamation point being used as a key in a lock.

3. *Choose a favorite actor and role and use the first letter of each word.* Again, you can use info-chaining. If you chose "Jimmy Stewart in" *It's a Wonderful Life*, you would have jsi-iawl. For additional security, you could capitalize the *a*. Then using the simple alphabet image of "ape" for *a*, you could come up with an image such as the following: Jimmy Stewart fishing the angel Clarence out of the river and discovering he's an ape. That image would make the choice memorable and lock the association into your brain.

Now, speaking of brains, go give yours a rest.

PART 4

Students
and Other
Learners

Hitting the Books

In this country we start studying, officially, at the age of five or six. For the next twelve years, while nature intended us to be out gathering nuts and berries and learning to hunt, we study for six to seven hours a day plus homework. Then many of us sign on for another four, six, or even eight years. And some of us get jobs that require us to keep studying, to some degree or another, for the rest of our working lives.

And most of us have no idea how to do it.

Speak for yourself, Jon.
Really? Can you honestly say that you know how to study, that you're satisfied with how well you read material and remember what you've read?

I wouldn't say satisfied. I get by.
Most of us do get by, but that's about all. We're never actually taught *how* to study. This absolutely crucial skill is simply not covered effectively in schools. One reason it isn't is that *memorization* has become a dirty word, educationally speaking.

It was certainly never my favorite part of school.
That's understandable. Most of us had trouble memorizing things in school.

The fact is, for a number of reasons, memorization has fallen into disrepute with those educators who prefer to encourage imagination, originality, and critical-thinking skills. For one thing, most people think there's only one kind of memorization—*rote* memorization. And that technique is so horribly inefficient that it really isn't worth the time and effort it takes, not to mention that it is so boring that it squelches a student's love of learning.

Let's face it—these days, with the ever-growing wealth of information that we can access instantly on the internet, students are more likely to be taught how to *find* the information they need than how to commit that information to memory.

That's understandable.
Sure it is. But it ignores the ancient and continuous connections between memory and the most creative aspects of human life.

Unlike computers, human beings do not simply store facts for future retrieval. We use anything and everything we've ever learned, constantly and imaginatively, every moment of our lives. It's absurd to suggest that anyone can come up with creative solutions to problems and interesting ideas to explore and then, when the time comes, "look up" whatever data he or she needs. Our own knowledge is part of the raw material of our creativity.

And don't forget that poetry, storytelling, and songs all came out of our need to remember. In a sense, we might even say that imagination developed so that we could remember things.

That's a pretty strong statement.
I know it is, but I've read a lot about the history of memory and memory training and I'll stand by it. The Greeks officially

recognized the fact by making Mnemosyne, the goddess of Memory, the mother of the muses.

So you're saying that making kids memorize stuff in class will make them more creative?
I'm saying that we should stop being *afraid* of memorization.

For one thing, most of us spend a lot of time daydreaming, like when we're riding on the bus or a commuter train, when we're sitting in a waiting room or in a doctor's examination room. It doesn't hurt to have our minds nicely furnished with a favorite poem or two, an interesting lecture or newspaper article to think about, instead of our money problems, for example.

I thought we were talking about studying.
That, too. Knowledge and understanding are both crucial to a good education, and we can't *know* something unless we remember it. So that's what we're going to work on, remembering what we've learned.

FOURTEEN

If You Can Read It, You Can Remember It

When you're studying, do you underline things in your text or maybe highlight them with a yellow marker? You know how that gives you the feeling that you're really learning the material? And you know how, later, you can't remember a quarter of what you've highlighted?

You bet you do. We all do. We feel as though the very act of marking the material is enough to help us remember—but it isn't, not really. It just makes it a little easier to find specific facts when we read the material over again. Well, what if everything you highlighted became part of your long-term memory?

Would that be great or what?

That's what my super-element technique is about. It gives you the ability to retain the important elements of anything you read. Memorizing lists using the idea-catcher technique is easy and kind of fun, and it can help in science classes where you have to remember the major systems of the human body or the chemical elements. But most of the information you'll read and want to remember in your lifetime—even what you'll learn in school—won't come in list form. It'll be served up to you in sentences, paragraphs, and chapters. You'll have to understand it and put it in context, as well as commit it to memory. And you'll be required to use the information, not just know it. The super-element method makes retaining what you read a fairly simple process. With it, you can remember anything you can understand.

> *A memory is what is left when something happens and does not completely unhappen.*
>
> **EDWARD DE BONO**

That's a crucial point. This method is not useful for rote memorization. If you can't understand the material in the first place, you're going to need some other method to remember it. The super-element method is, like any other association technique, simply designed to jumpstart your memory. You're going to create a whole bunch of little bouncers who will kick you smartly in the gray matter whenever you need them to. Your natural memory and your reading comprehension will take care of the rest.

Here's how it works. Read the following sentence:

Rubber bands last longer when they are refrigerated.

Now zero in on the super elements of the sentence. These will vary, sentence by sentence, depending on the context. In this case, having no context, I would choose these two:

rubber bands   refrigerated

These two elements form a very neat unit, a kind of bubble of information. And I will create an image that associates the two elements. Here's what I visualize:

a refrigerator completely wrapped in large rubber bands

You'll notice that I didn't need to add anything to my image about "lasting longer." I don't need it. When I picture the refrigerator wrapped in rubber bands, I will remember the way the two things are related. Here's another bit of information to add to your store:

The giant squid has the largest eyes in the world.

The elements I would choose here are:

> giant squid   large eyes

I don't need to include "in the world" any more than I need to include "has." The image I visualize here is:

a giant squid's tentacles wrapped around a huge eyeball

You get the idea? Try the method in the following exercise.

Memory Exercise #26

Choose two or three important elements in the following sentences. Then create an image for each sentence that associates those elements in some outlandish, but memorable, way.

1. The largest landowner in the world is McDonald's.
2. The Liberty Bell was so named in honor of slaves seeking their freedom.
3. The average American will eat half a ton of cheese in a lifetime.
4. Andrew Jackson held parties in the White House to which he invited everyone who wanted to attend.
5. A Venus flytrap can eat a cheeseburger.
6. Coca-Cola has the largest fleet of trucks in the world.
7. The only real person ever to have her head on a Pez dispenser was Betsy Ross.

8. There are more chickens than people.
9. Peanuts are one of the ingredients of dynamite.
10. Honeybees have hair on their eyes.

Possible Choices

Here are some quick associations I came up with:

1. the Golden Arches pulling "For Sale" signs out of the ground
2. the Liberty Bell being carried through the night by an escaping slave
3. Uncle Sam putting a wheel of cheese on one side of a balancing scale and a half-ton weight on the other side
4. Jack's son standing at the door of the White House shouting "Y'all come"
5. a Venus flytrap eating a cheeseburger
6. a fleet of trucks driven by Coke bottles
7. a Pez container stitching an American flag
8. a bunch of chickens marching around a person, with signs reading, "We're #1"
9. an exploding peanut
10. a bee sitting in a barber's chair saying, "Just a little around the iris"

All right, now let's try something a trifle more historical, say, the first sentences of a paragraph that comes from a brief history of bowling in *The Rule Book*, by the Diagram Group.

"Target games involving throwing a ball at a target of pins or skittles have a long history dating back to ancient Egypt."

These are the elements I would choose from that sentence in that context.

target games   ancient Egypt

As I said, choosing the super elements is a personal thing, like taking notes. There's no right or wrong way to do it. In this case, because I know that I'm reading about bowling, or throwing a ball at pins, I don't feel the need to include that element. So I have just two super elements to associate.

Remember that your two basic tools in this method are the element and the unit. The element is any point that makes an immediate impression on your mind. The unit is the two elements linked by an association.

Here's my image for this first sentence:

King Tut with a target painted on his chest

With that image safely tucked into my memory, I go on to the next sentence.

"Much later, European settlers took skittles games to North America, and it was in the U.S.A. in the nineteenth century that the modern competitive sport of tenpin bowling developed."

I'd choose the following five elements. Take a look at them and see whether they're what you would choose. They don't have to be, of course, but it can be instructive to compare.

European settlers   skittles   North America
nineteenth century   modern bowling

I'd use these elements to create two images, two information bubbles to float into my natural memory.

Pilgrims rolling a ball at the North American continent

lady wearing a bustle and a bowling shirt

Let me guess what you're thinking right now. "This could take forever!" or something along those lines. There are several reasons you're feeling that way. First, I'm explaining the method to you step by step, and it takes longer to explain it than to do it. Second, you're just learning the technique and everything takes longer in the beginning. As you come to trust your memory, you will use fewer and less elaborate reminders. Third, using this technique *does* take longer than simply reading. But it doesn't take much longer, once you've practiced it a little, and it pays off big-time. You will never forget the history of bowling, for example. Using this method to study for a final exam will mean a fairly brief and *productive* review of the material, instead of a largely futile cram session.

Let's just finish this paragraph on bowling and see what other kinds of challenges it offers.

"Centers were built in many U.S. cities during the course of the century, but not until after the formation of the American Bowling Congress (ABC) in 1895 was there a standardization of rules and equipment."

We already know what the first part of the sentence tells us, so I went on to the second part. Here are the elements I'd choose for this rather long statement:

American Bowling Congress   1895 standardization

A date. What are we going to do with a date? In some cases, exact dates are not important. In those cases, you could use an image related to the late nineteenth century. But if you want to recall the specific date, you can use the number/sound system. I wouldn't bother with the whole number myself. You know from the get-go that nothing related to bowling happened in America in A.D. 895, so you don't have to bother with the *1*. Substituting the sounds for *895* could give you the word *feeble*. With that in mind, I would come up with this image:

> *a bunch of standardized (identical) Congressmen bowling feebly*

How I handled the date in the last sentence is an example of how this method works. You can use any or all of the skills you've learned so far in conjunction with the super elements. You choose the elements and skills you'll use.

The important thing is to create a visual context for the material as you read. If you do that, your mind will turn your comprehension into retention. In other words, what you've read won't go flying out of your brain the moment you put the book down.

I hear and I forget. I see and I remember. I do and I understand.

CONFUCIUS

Now remember that you're not translating this material into code. You don't have to hit on every detail. In fact, one of the best ways to use the super-element method is to memorize your class notes. If you're a reasonably good note taker, what you've written as you listen to a lecture are your elements. Later, you can transform those elements into images, using the basic understanding you gained from listening to the whole lecture as the glue or context that holds your elements together.

All right, here's one more sentence from the bowling paragraph. Try to decide how you would handle it before you look at my choices.

"Tenpin bowling remained an essentially U.S. sport until the middle of the century, when it began to acquire popularity elsewhere."

The point being made here is that bowling became popular in other countries around the middle of the century. My elements, therefore, are these:

middle of the century   popularity   outside U.S.

And here is my image:

people of all nations standing in the middle of a century note ($100 bill), cheering a bowling ball

Are you beginning to get the idea? My biggest problem in teaching this technique is that people get too linear, to use a current catchphrase. They want to include everything and structure all the elements so that they make perfect, logical sense. You just don't need to go that far. What you're going for are hints, cues, visual strings around your finger. You don't need to strive for perfection. It's irrelevant.

Okay, let's do another paragraph, this one from the Miami Museum of Science website.

"A hurricane is a powerful storm that measures several hundred miles in diameter. Hurricanes have two main parts. The first is the eye of the hurricane, which is a calm area in the center of the storm. Usually, the eye of a hurricane measures about 20 miles in diameter, and has very few clouds. The second part is the wall of clouds that surrounds the calm eye. This is where the hurricane's strongest winds and heaviest rain occur."

Once you've read the entire paragraph, go through it sentence by sentence to choose your super elements. After you've done that, take a look at the elements I chose, just for comparison. Remember, my choices are not the *correct* choices. They're just *my* choices, but they may be useful in helping you master the technique.

powerful storm	several hundred miles
eye	calm
20 miles	few clouds
wall of clouds	strong winds and rain

Now these are the images I came up with for the elements I chose.

a storm cloud making a muscle and standing by a road that stretches hundreds of miles into the distance

an eye sitting calmly in a lotus position

a large eye chart (20/20 vision) with a scattering of clouds floating by

a wall made of clouds laid like bricks being battered by winds and rain

All right, let's see if you're ready to try an exercise on your own.

Memory Exercise #27

Read this paragraph from the University of Michigan Museum of Zoology's Animal Diversity website. Try using the number/sound system for the numbers in the excerpt.

"The approximately 925 species of living bats make up around 20% of all known living mammal species. In some tropical areas, there are more species of bats than of all other kinds of mammals combined. Bats are found throughout the world in tropical and temperate habitats. They are missing only from polar regions and from some isolated islands."

Possible Choices

Elements:

925 species
20% of mammals
tropical   more species   other mammals
no bats   polar regions

Images:

a secret panel (an image for 925 using the number/sound system) on Noah's ark (all different species)

a furry (mammal) nose (an image for 20 using the number/sound system) on a penny (cent)

a palm tree on a second ark, which is filled with bats

a globe covered with bats except at the top and bottom

I hope the super-element method is starting to feel comfortable for you. I can't emphasize enough how useful it is. I've taught it to all kinds of people, from medical students who use it to memorize vast quantities of technical material, to business executives who use it to remain up to speed on developments in the corporate world. Even though some find it a bit strange at first, virtually anyone who is motivated can master it quickly. And once it becomes second nature, you'll be able to remember anything you study so well that it will amaze you. I know, because the technique is actually a refinement of the memory method I used all during college and ended up teaching my professors.

It works.

All right, just to give you a little practice, I'm going to give you a few more paragraphs to work with. You'll notice that I didn't write any of these myself. I didn't design them to make the super-element method look better or work more easily. I found the material in books and websites that you might find yourself. The exercises are arranged in order of difficulty, from easy to advanced.

Memory Exercise #28

Read this paragraph from the *Sunset Western Garden Book*, by the editors of Sunset Books and *Sunset Magazine*.

"Aphids are soft, oval, pinhead-to-match-head-sized insects that huddle together on new shoots, buds, and leaves. They come in many colors—including green, pink, red, and black—with and without wings."

"Numerous creatures keep aphid populations in check; often the best tactic is to do nothing and watch natural controls go to work. . . . If you spray with a toxic insecticide, you risk killing the insect predators along with the problem. Fortunately, you can get rid of most aphids with a blast of water from the hose."

Memory Exercise #29

Read this paragraph from *The World Factbook*, published by the Central Intelligence Agency of the United States.

"A Slavic state, Bulgaria achieved independence in 1908 after 500 years of Ottoman rule. Bulgaria fought on the losing side in both World Wars. After World War II it fell within the Soviet sphere of influence. Communist domination ended in 1991 with the dissolution of the USSR, and Bulgaria began the contentious process of moving toward political democracy and a market economy. In addition to the problems of structural economic reform, particularly privatization, Bulgaria faces the serious issues of keeping inflation and unemployment under control, combating corruption, and curbing black-market and mafia-style crime."

Memory Exercise #30

Read this paragraph from *Introduction to Music*, by Hugh M. Miller.

"All musical tone consists of four properties: (1) pitch, (2) duration, (3) intensity, and (4) quality. PITCH. The term *pitch* refers to the highness or lowness of a tonal sound. It is a physical principle that the faster the vibrations are, the higher the pitch will be, and the slower the vibrations, the lower the pitch. The human ear can detect pitches as low as 16 vibrations per second and as high as 20,000 vibrations per second. The tones of the piano, an instrument which includes almost all the pitches found in music, range from 30 to 4,000 vibrations per second."

It is estimated by scientists that millions of trees are accidentally planted by squirrels who bury nuts and then forget where they hid them.

---- **FIFTEEN** ----

What's the Word?

I don't know of anything that will help you more in your studies than having an outstanding vocabulary. I'm not talking about throwing around six-syllable words to impress people. I'm talking about using words that will help you communicate exactly what you mean, words that convey your message with precision and power. A great vocabulary will also help you to get much more out of anything you read.

To acquire this sort of vocabulary, you don't need to work through lists of antonyms and synonyms. Most of us encounter all the vocabulary words we will ever need to master in the course of our everyday conversation and reading. We just don't remember them.

That's where I can help you. My purpose in this chapter is to help you *remember* the meaning of a term or word that is new to you. There are four steps in this process.

1. Look up the meaning of the word. Ask someone what it means, or figure out the meaning from the context.
2. Analyze the structure of the word. Notice any prefixes, roots, and suffixes. Fix the meaning of the word in your mind by seeing how it is reflected in the word's structure.

3. Pay attention to the word in context. The context can help you remember the word later.
4. Use the sound of the word and/or its meaning to create an image that will help you remember it.

The last step is my own special contribution, of course. I'm not going to let you get by without some visualization and association work. In fact, for some words, that will be your primary memory tool. But let's begin with a few words that will give you a chance to practice all four steps.

Suppose, for example, that you're reading and you encounter the word *pellucid*, as in, "Henry James's ornate, almost perversely complex style is far from pellucid." When you look the word up, you'll find that it means "completely clear, transparent." When you analyze the structure of the word, you'll see that it contains the root word *lucid*, which you probably already know means "clear in the mind." That should help you fix the meaning. The sentence as a whole describes a writer's very fancy style, so the context gives you a sense that the word has something to do with simplicity. Your last step is to create an image that will help you commit the definition to memory. You might imagine a pellucid *pel*ican as one you can *see right through*.

Athazagoraphobia is the fear of being forgotten or ignored—or of forgetting something.

Let's take another example. "The once-bright star of daytime television has fallen, because of his actions, into ignominy." When you look up *ignominy*, you'll discover that it means "disgrace or dishonor." When you analyze the structure of the word, you'll see that it contains the root *nom*, which means "name" and the prefix *ig-*, which means "no." That structure wouldn't tell you what the word means, but since you've already looked up the definition, what you know about the structure can help you fix it in your memory. A person who was once proud of his name now has been shamed. The context gives you a sense of a fall from light to darkness, a nice visual image. For the last step, the memory image, you might imagine *many* people *ignor*ing someone who has fallen into ignominy.

Memory Exercise #31

Try the method yourself on the italicized words in these sentences. Remember, look the word up, analyze it, pay attention to the context, and create an image. Your "dictionary" appears after the sentences. I put the words in alphabetical order so it'll seem just like a real dictionary, except that you can't use it for a doorstop.

Herman was the only member of the group who had the *prescience* to prepare for rain, so the rest of us got soaked.

We soon came to see Elisa's *vagaries* as amusing, except when she got it into her head that she must have licorice ice cream at midnight.

His sense of history was so bad that he thought Franklin Roosevelt was *contemporaneous* with Benjamin Franklin.

Beth called it music, but her father called it *cacophony*.

Kim begged for forgiveness, but Melissa was completely *implacable*.

Paolo's love for bright colors led him to collect *polychrome* pottery.

DICTIONARY

cacophony (kuh KOF uh nee), *n.* harsh, unharmonious sound.

contemporaneous (kuhn TEM puh RAY nee us), *adj.* [Latin *contemporaneus*, from *com-*, same + *tempus*, time] existing, living, or occurring at the same time.

implacable (im PLAK uh bul), *adj.* [Latin *implacabilis*, from *in-*, not + *placabilis*, easily calmed] not to be appeased or pacified.

polychrome (POHL ee KROM), *adj.* [Greek *polychromos*, from *poly-*, many + *chroma*, colors] multicolored.

prescience (PREH shee ens), *n.* [from Latin *prae-*, before + *scire*, to know] advance knowledge; foresight.

vagary (VA guh ree), *n.* [from Latin *vagari*, to wander] an unpredictable or extravagant action or notion.

An autobiography usually reveals nothing bad about its writer except his memory.

FRANKLIN P. JONES

Possible Image Choices

These are the images I visualized for each word:

prescience	fortune-teller seeing precious stones in your future
vagaries	a vague-looking Aries dancing in the street
contemporaneous	two con artists born at the same time (twins), dancing in the rain
cacophony	a bunch of phonies cackling and coughing

implacable	Abel painted on a plaque looking unforgivingly toward Cain
polychrome	Polly parrot made of many colors of chrome

Of course, there are times when you won't have a dictionary with you, at least not one that gives you word origins. In that case, it can be useful to know the meanings of common roots and affixes. Often, when you detect a Latin or Greek word part in a word, you can get pretty close to its meaning by searching your mind for another word with the same root. If you come across *retrogress*, for example, you might recognize the root *gress* from *progress*. Chances are you could guess that it means "go" or something close to that. Since we all know what *retro* means these days, you could figure out that *retrogress* means "go backward," and proceed from there to follow the four steps in the memory technique.

However, that method won't always work, so it's useful to be familiar with some of the more common word parts. For each root or prefix in the following lists, I created an absurd and therefore memorable image using:

- a familiar word that contains that word part, or
- an action or situation that suggests the meaning of the word part.

After you've taken a look at these, you can create a few more associations yourself.

ROOT WORDS

Word Part	*Meaning*	*Image*
port	carry	a porter *carry*ing a *port*hole
nom, nym	name	a huge *name* tag *nom*inating a candidate at a presidential convention

gen	give birth	a pregnant woman sitting in a family tree, or *gen*ealogical chart
greg	flock	a *flock* of geese forming the con-*greg*ation in a church one Sunday morning, to the astonishment of the pastor
chron	time	a bunch of clocks doing syn*chro*nized swimming
mim	imitate	a *mim*e trying to *imitate* a mimeograph machine

PREFIXES

Word Part	*Meaning*	*Image*
tele	distant	a shot-putter hurling a *tele*vision a great *distance*
ambi, amphi	two	*two* equally ugly *amphi*bians, or frogs
bene	good	Jack Benny wearing a halo and smiling *bene*volently
circum	around	a clown riding a bicycle *around* a *circus* ring until he falls down
com, con	together	a *com*mittee trying to walk down the street *together*, in step with each other
mal	bad	a very *bad* apple *mal*iciously ru-ining a whole barrel, laughing the whole while
omni	all	a cartoon *omni*bus stopping at *all* the stops on the route
pseudo	false	a writer in a huge *false* mustache signing a *pseudo*nym
trans	across, beyond	a *Trans*World Airlines plane tiptoeing *across* a road

Memory Exercise #32

Now that you're familiar with this technique, see if you can create images for these word parts. To give you a start, I've added to the list a few vocabulary words that contain each word part. Create your memory image using these words or any other words you happen to know with the same word part. Remember to use the imagination stimulators—exaggeration, substitution, and motion.

PREFIXES

Word Part	Meaning	Vocabulary
ab, abs	away, off	absent, abscond, abdicate, abduct, abnormal
ante	before	anteroom, antebellum, antedate
contra	against, opposite	contrary, contrast, contradict
e, ex	out of, from	exit, excavate, exclude
crypto	hidden, secret	crypt, cryptogram, cryptic
neo	new	neon, neophyte, neoclassical

ROOT WORDS

Word Part	Meaning	Vocabulary
tort	twist	distort, torture, retort
fac, fec	make or do	manufacture, effect, faction
dur	hard	enduring, durable, duress
lumen, luc	light	illuminate, lucid, elucidate, lucite
sat	enough	satisfy, sated

Possible Choices

ab, abs	Abbott running *away* from Costello as he *absconds* with all the loot
ante	a bunch of aunties who arrived at the party *before* everyone else, waiting in the *anteroom*
contra	two huge professional wrestlers wearing *contrasting* colors pushing *against* each other
e, ex	Liz Taylor and all her *exes* rushing *out* the fire *exit* at a movie theater
crypto	Lex Luthor gloating over the *secret* supply of *Kryptonite* he keeps in a *crypt*
neo	a huge red *neon* sign flashing, "*New! New! New!*"
tort	a *tortoise* doing the *twist* with a hare
fac, fec	Willie Wonka's chocolate *factory making* huge bricks of chocolate
dur	an *endurance* contest between a rock and a *hard* place
lumen, luc	Luke Skywalker using a *light* stick made out of *lucite*
sat	feeling *dissatisfied* because you just *sat* in a pie

Of course, there are a lot of words in the English language that do not have roots and prefixes and still others where the word parts are too obscure to be useful as memory aids. With those words, you can simply skip that step in the process. Here's a list to practice on.

Memory Exercise #33

Look up the meaning of each of the highlighted words in the sentences below. Pay attention to the context of each word, and create an image that will help you remember it.

1. At home, Gregory seemed proud and self-reliant, but in the office he was revealed to be little more than a *sycophant*.

2. A good administrator must have *acumen* as well as power.
3. While many Americans participate fully in our affluent society, others live in *penury*.
4. The screwball comedies of the 1930s were marked by a kind of *badinage* we seem to have lost the knack for.
5. Buster Keaton's *doleful* face has, ironically, been the cause of great laughter for generations.
6. Although he was quiet, there was nothing *furtive* about his actions.
7. Before receiving the *plaudits* of the critics, Sarah accepted the congratulations of her fellow actors.
8. Any dentist will tell you to *eschew* sugary treats, especially sticky ones.

DICTIONARY

acumen (ah KYOO men), *n.* the ability to make judgments quickly and well, especially in practical matters.

badinage (BAHD in AHJ), *n.* playful banter.

doleful (DOL ful), *adj.* filled with great sadness.

eschew (ess CHEW), *v.* to avoid consistently, especially for moral or practical reasons.

furtive (FUR tiv), *adj.* characterized by secrecy and guile.

penury (PEN yah ree), *n.* extreme poverty.

plaudit (PLAW dit), *n.* enthusiastic praise—usually used in the plural (plaudits).

sycophant (SIK ah fant), *n.* a self-seeking flatterer.

Possible Choices

sycophant	sick elephant giving compliments
acumen	a cue man (pool stick) giving good advice to a younger guy

penury	a giant penny dressed as a shopping-bag lady
badinage	two large bandages engaged in witty conversation
doleful	a large Dole pineapple crying
furtive	a fugitive sneaking around
plaudits	giant claws clapping
eschew	an Eskimo chewing and avoiding you

A final note. I've already mentioned the power of story-telling in memory. One of the very best ways to remember a word is to learn a story about it. Here are two stories that will probably cement some words into your vocabulary forever:

The ancient Greek city-state of Sparta was once known as Laconia. Its citizens were reputed to be tough warriors and, in temperament, a lot like Dirty Harry. They were noted, in particular, for their economy of language. According to legend, when Philip of Macedonia was storming the gates of Laconia (or Sparta), he sent a message to the king that said, "If we capture your city, we will burn it to the ground." The king replied *laconically*, "If."

Cyrano de Bergerac, the hero of a play by French writer Edmond Rostand, was well known for his abnormally large nose—but equally for his dashing style, his nerve, and his elegant wit. Cyrano's *panache* was evident when, after winning a duel (during which he simultaneously composed poetry), he graciously pardoned his defeated foe with a flamboyant sweep of his hat and its large plume—also called a *panache*.

A goldfish has a memory span of three seconds.

SIXTEEN

Underlining in Your Mind

Brace yourself. You're about to make an investment of time and energy that will pay off in a big, big way if you're

- a student
- a teacher
- someone who has to do a lot of reading on the job, or
- a writer or researcher

This method could make an enormous difference in your efficiency and productivity. On the other hand, you should probably skip this chapter if you

- hated the number/sound system; or
- rarely need to commit specific information to memory.

It's going to take some work and, if you don't do the exercises, there isn't much point in reading it. It won't hurt you, of course, but you may find it a little strange.

In chapter 8 you learned how to use the idea catchers to memorize lists of ten or fewer items. Then, in chapter 9, you learned about the number/sound system. Now you're going to learn how to combine those two systems to commit to memory a long list of items—an infinite number, in theory.

Three things are bad for you. I can't remember the first two, but doughnuts are the third.

BILL PETERSEN

Like the idea catchers, this memory technique, called info-spacing, is developed from the Method of Loci. Each space in this system, however, is occupied by an image that is based on the number's sound equivalent in the number/sound system, rather than on its similarity in shape to a number. Because the number 1 in the number/sound system corresponds to *T*, the first image is *tea*. The number 2 corresponds to *N*, so the first image is a word in which *N* is the only consonant sound: *Noah*. The number 3, in my system, is *May*, a word in which *M* is the only consonant sound. And the number 4 is *hare*, a word in which *R* is the only consonant sound.

Now, don't be confused because *R* is not the first letter of that word. Remember that *H* doesn't count as a consonant in the number/sound system. I could have chosen a word that began with *R*, but my options are severely limited. *Ray* is too much like *X-ray*, which I want to use for *X*, and there aren't a lot of other good choices. I mean, *roe* means "fish eggs," and how useful is that when you're trying to make striking, memorable info-chains? So just accept the fact that a few of these words don't look at first glance as though they conform to the number/sound system, and you'll be fine.

The info-space memory technique has been around for centuries, and the images have been developed with two criteria—ease of learning and memorability. The secret of its success is that once you've learned the number/sound equivalents and the image linked to each, you can use that framework to remember any number of items.

All memory trainers have used this method because it works

so well, and all employ time-tested images. The images used may vary from trainer to trainer, however, so feel free to replace any one of the images I'm suggesting with something that works better for you. After all, it's your memory. However, you'll probably want to stick with most of my suggestions.

Whenever I present this method these days, I think of a young man who came to one of my memory seminars. I called him the Karate Kid because he was a martial arts student. He told me he was having a lot of trouble remembering the proper sequence for all the positions he needed to do in order to qualify for his black belt. He used the info-space method to fix the sequence in his mind until the various positions became second nature to him. It worked like a charm.

All right, I want you to look at the first ten info-spaces. We'll do a few exercises with them and then go on to others. Read through the list and create a visual image for each word.

INFO-SPACES 1–10

1 = Tea (T)
2 = Noah (N)
3 = May (M)
4 = Hare (R)
5 = Wall (L)
6 = Shoe (J)
7 = Key (K)
8 = Wave (V)
9 = Pa (P)
10 = Dice (S)

When I use these info-spaces, tea is represented by a tea bag. Noah, of course, is the biblical figure, a bearded man in a robe, standing in front of an ark. May is a calendar page with spring flowers on it. Hare is a rabbit. Wall is usually a brick wall, but it can vary. My image of a shoe is a running shoe. My key is an old-fashioned skeleton key. To fill out the rest of the info-spaces, I visualize an ocean wave, a father, and a pair of dice.

Now read through the list once again to become more familiar with the visual equivalents. Okay? Now we can try an exercise. As you did with the idea catchers, you're going to create an image for whatever you want to remember and then link it to the info-space image by association.

Memory Exercise #34

Create a visual image that associates each of the following U.S. presidents with the appropriate info-space.

1. Washington
2. Adams
3. Jefferson
4. Madison
5. Monroe
6. Adams (Quincy)
7. Jackson
8. Van Buren
9. Harrison (William)
10. Tyler

Possible Choices

Did you make your images ridiculous enough to remember? Here's my list, just for comparison.

1. Washington	George hanging up freshly washed tea bags
2. Adams	Noah floating the ark over a series of dams
3. Jefferson	a calendar page trying to choose between Jeff or his son
4. Madison	a hare getting mad at his son
5. Monroe	Marilyn Monroe jumping over a brick wall

6. Adams (Quincy)	a shoe floating over a series of dams made of cue sticks
7. Jackson	Jack's son climbing a tall key instead of a beanstalk
8. Van Buren	a wave crashing over a buried van
9. Harrison (William)	a hairy father holding his son and signing his will
10. Tyler	a pair of big foam dice tied together

Okay, close the book. See how many of these first ten presidents you can remember in order. Then go back over the list of presidents one more time before you move on. Remind yourself of the ones you were not able to recall. Then if you review the list tomorrow and again five days from now, the information should be yours to keep.

So far, this system doesn't have any appreciable advantage over the idea catchers. But it doesn't end with just ten spaces. I'm going to give you info-space visual elements for the numbers up to 50. You can create your own info-space for any number at all, using the number/sound system to designate each digit of the number, with a word derived from its corresponding sound.

Now, just to get the old synapses snapping, here's a memory joke.

An elephant and a crocodile are hanging out at the old watering hole when the elephant sees a turtle sitting on a nearby rock. The elephant galumphs over, picks up the turtle, and throws him into the jungle.

"Why'd you do that?" the crocodile asks.

"That turtle bit me once fifty years ago."

"Wow," says the crocodile. "You must have a great memory."

"You bet," the elephant says. "I have turtle recall."

And now, a break.

Do something with a friend.

All right, read through this list of the next ten info-spaces. You'll note that all the numbers 11–19 are associated with items that begin with the letter *T* because 1 is represented by *T* in the number/sound system. The second sound in each word corresponds, again, to its phonetic equivalent in the number/sound system.

Now visualize an image for each item. Then try to recall the images from memory. Read through the list again once to reinforce what you learned, and remind yourself of any item you missed the first time.

INFO-SPACES 11–20

   11 = Toad
   12 = Tin
   13 = Tomb
   14 = Tar
   15 = Tail
   16 = Tissue
   17 = Tack
   18 = Taffy

19 = Tub
20 = Nose

If you've gone through the list twice, go on to the next memory exercise, right after you take a break.

Go shopping.

If you're working along with me, by the time you've finished this chapter, you'll have memorized all the presidents of the United States, in chronological order. This is not just a parlor trick, and it's not *just* a handy way to teach you the info-spacing technique. From now on, every time you hear or read a piece of information about one of these presidents, you'll have a feeling for how that information fits into our country's history. It's a good example of how memorization can enhance learning—so long as it's not rote memorization, which bores the learning right out of you.

So on to the next exercise and then I'll tell you another joke. I promise.

Memory Exercise #35

Create a visual image that associates each of the following with the appropriate info-space. These are the U.S. presidents, 11 through 20.

11. Polk
12. Taylor
13. Fillmore
14. Pierce
15. Buchanan
16. Lincoln
17. Johnson
18. Grant
19. Hayes
20. Garfield

Possible Choices

How did you do? Did you remember to use exaggeration, substitution, and motion to create your images? They're real aids to memory. Here are my choices:

11.	Polk	a huge finger poking a toad
12.	Taylor	a tailor sewing a suit out of tin
13.	Fillmore	a tomb filled with more and more funeral wreaths
14.	Pierce	a Pierce-Arrow car stuck in hot tar
15.	Buchanan	a cannon with a tiger's tail
16.	Lincoln	a Lincoln log cabin overflowing with tissue
17.	Johnson	John's son about to sit on a tack
18.	Grant	a grant written on sticky taffy
19.	Hayes	a bathtub full of hay
20.	Garfield	Garfield the cat sleeping on a huge nose

Now close the book and try to remember this group of presidents in order. Then read over this second list again, just once. Remind yourself of the presidents you were unable to recall with the book closed. To seal the list in your memory, review it again tomorrow, and once again five days from now.

All right, here's the joke I promised.

Three people are taking a memory test. The first man is suffering from sleep deprivation. The psychologist asks him, "What's three times three?"

The guy says, "596."

The second man was a prizefighter in his youth. The psychologist asks him, "What's three times three?"

The guy says, "Tuesday."

So the psychologist turns to the third person, a woman who keeps forgetting to take her ginkgo. "What's three times three?" he asks.

"Nine," she answers.

"That's right!" says the doctor. "Now tell me how you got that number."

"Easy," says the woman. "I subtracted 596 from Tuesday."

Okay, it's time for a break. Then we'll go on to the rest of the info-spaces and more presidents.

Make some music.

Back already? Raring to go? Okay, read through the following list once, visualizing as you go. Close the book and try to remember the images. Then read through the list again, to reinforce the associations and remind yourself of any that you missed. When you're ready, go on to the next exercise.

INFO-SPACES 21–30

21 = Net

22 = Nanny

23 = Name (business card)
24 = Winner
25 = Nail
26 = Wench
27 = Ink
28 = Navy
29 = Nip
30 = Mice

Memory Exercise #36

Here are presidents 21 to 30. Create an image for each one, and don't spare anyone's dignity. If you can't remember the image for any given number, try recalling it by assigning sounds to the digits. If you can't remember the image for 25, for example, think *N* and *L* and see if you come up with *nail*.

21. Arthur
22. Cleveland
23. Harrison (Benjamin)
24. Cleveland
25. McKinley
26. Roosevelt (Theodore)
27. Taft
28. Wilson
29. Harding
30. Coolidge

Possible Choices

Once again, I offer up my images to help stimulate your imagination.

21. Arthur   King Arthur and the Round Table
                    trapped in a huge net

22.	Cleveland	a sweet little nanny wielding a large cleaver
23.	Harrison (Benj.)	a hairy son (little boy) exchanging business cards with Big Ben
24.	Cleveland	a cleaver wearing a blue ribbon
25.	McKinley	a nail as tall as Mt. McKinley
26.	Roosevelt (T.)	a wench setting up a golf tee in a field of roses
27.	Taft	a daft writer throwing ink everywhere
28.	Wilson	Will's son running away to join the Navy
29.	Harding	someone taking a nip at a hard candy and breaking a tooth
30.	Coolidge	a very cool mouse, shivering

Close the book now and try to remember this group of presidents in order. Then read over the list of presidents again,

just once. Remind yourself of the ones you missed. For best retention, review the list a day from now and five days later.

Count a few sheep.

Moving right along, here are the next ten info-spaces. Read through the list once, visualizing as you go. When you're ready, close the book and try to recall the images. Then read through the list again to remind yourself of the ones you missed and reinforce what you've learned. Then go on to the exercise.

Memory Exercise #37

INFO-SPACES 31–40

31 = Maid
32 = Money
33 = Mummy
34 = Mayor
35 = Mill
36 = Match
37 = Mike
38 = Movie
39 = Map
40 = Rice

Do some light reading.

Memory Exercise #38

Another ten presidents. Whoopee!!

31. Hoover
32. Roosevelt (Franklin)
33. Truman
34. Eisenhower
35. Kennedy

36. Johnson
37. Nixon
38. Ford
39. Carter
40. Reagan

Possible Choices

What did you come up with for these? Here's my list:

31.	Hoover	a maid using a Hoover vacuum cleaner
32.	Roosevelt (F.)	a large rose bush with a pile of Franklins ($100 bills) under it for mulch
33.	Truman	a mummy in court swearing to tell the truth
34.	Eisenhower	a mayor holding an hourglass sideways, with eyes where the glass bulges
35.	Kennedy	a water mill pouring out Kennedy half dollars
36.	Johnson	anyone named John striking a match that makes a flame as big and bright as the sun
37.	Nixon	a bunch of little St. Nicks atop a microphone
38.	Ford	a movie cameraman shooting film while riding in a model-T Ford
39.	Carter	a cart traveling along a road as pictured on a map
40.	Reagan	a ray-gun shooting rice

Once again, close the book and try to remember this group of presidents in order. Then read over the list, just once, reminding yourself of the ones you had some trouble with. Use the one-day, two-day, five-day review technique to lock this sequence in memory.

One more joke.

A wildly upset man ran into a psychiatrist's office. "Doctor," he cried, "my memory's gone. I can't remember anything. I don't know my wife's name or my kids' names. I've forgotten where I live and what kind of car I drive. You've got to help me!"

"Just calm down," said the psychiatrist. "How long have you been this way?"

"What way?"

Play with your dog.

All right, the last set of ten info-spaces. Read through it once, of course, creating your memorable images. Then review the list before going on to the exercise.

INFO-SPACES 41–50

   41 = Rat
   42 = Rain
   43 = Ram
   44 = Roar
   45 = Rail
   46 = Rash
   47 = Rug
   48 = Roof
   49 = Robe
   50 = Lace

Memory Exercise #39

You didn't think I'd stop with Reagan, did you? Here are the last couple of presidents and my predictions up to number 50. (Don't worry. My specialty is the past, not the future. These predictions *will never come true*. Then again, you never know.)

41. Bush
42. Clinton
43. ???????
44. Ventura
45. Streisand
46. Schwarzenegger
47. Gates
48. Winfrey
49. Stephanopoulos
50. DiCaprio

Possible Choices

Did you have some fun with this set? I did. Here are my associations:

41. Bush	rats deserting a sinking bush
42. Clinton	a freshly cleaned ton weight getting caught in the rain
43. ???????	question marks painted on the side of a ram
44. Ventura	a huge roar coming out of a vent
45. Streisand	a train on dry sand (in a desert) instead of on rails
46. Schwarzenegger	a muscular egg in shorts, scratching a rash
47. Gates	a rolled-up rug walking through a gate

48. Winfrey   a big sign on a roof that reads "Win
                     Free Money!!"
49. Stephanopoulos   a stiff octopus in a robe
50. DiCaprio   a large D wearing a lace cap

Great Minds Think Alike

Happiness is nothing more than good health and a bad memory.

ALBERT SCHWEITZER

One of the keys to happiness is a bad memory.

ANATOLE FRANCE

A person is never happy except at the price of some ignorance.

RITA MAE BROWN

A lot of people mistake a short memory for a clear conscience.

DOUG LARSON

Happiness is good health and a bad memory.

INGRID BERGMAN

Memorize a Magazine

Did you ever try to memorize a magazine? Not every word, mind you. Just the sequence of articles and ads, the basic ideas presented, some of the more important supporting details, page by page.

Sound impossible? Not really. I do it all the time, whenever I'm looking for something extra to do with the super-elements and the info-spaces. When I demonstrate this technique on television talk shows, people usually find it remarkable.

Want to give it a shot? First, you need to get a magazine

that has a lot of photographs in it, say *Time* or *Newsweek*. I'll wait here.

Okay, open the magazine to a two-page spread with several pictures on it. Got it? Fine. Read through the two pages at a normal rate of speed. Now to remember what's on these pages, use the feature-scanning method you learned in Part I of this book, in the chapters on linking names and faces. Draw a Z across the spread with your eyes, beginning at the top of the lefthand page.

Now, I don't know what you're looking at right now. In my magazine, I'm looking at an advertisement for coffee on the lefthand page. It's a close-up shot of a white cup filled with steaming coffee. The cup, with its saucer and a spoon, is resting on an open book. On the righthand page there's a cartoon graph of the Dow-Jones average. The cartoon shows a bunch of happy investors riding the graph in a roller coaster car.

The first two elements I'm going to choose are the cup of coffee and the roller coaster car. To link these images and remember them, I'm going to imagine the investors riding up and down the graph in the cup. Then I'm going to focus on the steam rising from the cup of coffee and the Dow-Jones graph. I'll visualize the graph rising from the cup. Finally, I'll concentrate on the spoon that's resting on the saucer and the page number on the lefthand page. That is always the final step, linking the page number to an image on the page. The page number is 42. Using the number/sound system, I come up with *R* and *N* and turn them into the word *rain*. So my final image is that of a spoon dancing in the rain like Gene Kelly.

Using this method, I'm able to remember just what is on both pages of the magazine. I will have a remarkably clear sense of those pages. When I do this demonstration on television, I take the magazine backstage for one hour and go through it, spread by spread. Then when I come on stage, people call out random page numbers, and I'm able to recall what's on every page, one by one. I usually do the whole magazine.

And I never miss.

I'll never forget one of my former students, a physician who had taken four or five memory courses prior to this one in an attempt to become more efficient at processing the massive amount of new information he was expected to learn every week. The good doctor went through the entire workshop and did rather well. Then, just before the session ended, I showed the class how to memorize a magazine. The doctor was incredulous and insisted that the technique could not work.

He was determined to prove me wrong, so I dared him to give it a try and handed him an old copy of *Newsweek*. He disappeared into the hallway for several minutes and scanned the first forty pages or so. Then he stepped back into the conference room, holding the magazine in front of him at arm's length, cover closed. He continued to predict that the method wouldn't work, but when I called out a few page numbers at random, he was able to tell me exactly what appeared on every spread.

Suddenly he stopped, an amazed look on his face. He was so accustomed to memory courses *not* delivering everything they promised, he was startled when he realized that this one *had*.

PART 5

Young, Old, and In Between

SEVENTEEN

General Memory
Maintenance

The memory techniques in this book are useful for anyone—old or young, male or female, student or corporate executive. They are both time-tested and state of the art. They work.

But some of you may be wondering whether there are remedies for your special memory problems. If you're getting older, are there drugs or supplements you can take to rejuvenate a flagging memory? If you're a parent, is there anything special you can do to give your toddler a head start on developing a great memory?

As I've said before, memory training is the single most effective method for improving your memory. However, in this chapter, I'm going to tell you *everything else* I've learned about keeping your memory in good working order. I'm going to talk to you about nutrition, supplements, exercise, and memory games—all approaches that can help you keep your memory operating at cruising speed.

Before I go on, however, I'm going to ask you to turn the page and review the POPCORN Principles, seven easy rules your memory can live by. We introduced these principles earlier, but they're crucial to memory enhancement and can stand repeating. Why POPCORN? Look at the first letter of each rule.

THE POPCORN PRINCIPLES

Positive Attitude
Approach each memory challenge with a sense that you can meet it. Deliberately imagine the rewards for remembering in each case.

Observation
Notice your surroundings. Pay attention to what's going on around you.

Picturing
Use your ability to visualize. Visual memory is far more effective than verbal memory.

Concentration
Focus your attention. Don't let your mind wander from the memory task.

Organization
Organize the facts you have to remember. You will grasp them more quickly and retain them longer.

Review
Review material you want to remember by saying it out loud. Using the vocal cords stimulates natural memory.

Natural Association
Without going into info-spaces, idea catchers, and info-chains, you can simply use whatever associations come to mind spontaneously.

After POPCORN, we come, naturally enough, to food. There is no miracle food that will instantly boost your memory, but there are several nutrients essential to optimal brain function. These include many of the B vitamins, which are found in whole-grain breads, cereals, and some fruits and vegetables. Antioxidants repair and prevent damage to all of the cells in your body, including those in your brain. Vitamins A, C, and E are potent antioxidants.

You also need water. Of course, you've been hearing for years that you should drink eight glasses of water every day to keep your body in tip-top condition. Well, a lack of water has a profound negative effect on your brain. Dehydration causes confusion and short-term memory loss in no time at all.

Seems like I remember my mother telling me something like this. "Eat your vegetables. Drink a glass of water now and then."
Mom would agree with the next advice as well. Get enough sleep. Rest is crucial for the brain. When you're asleep, the brain doesn't have to bother about responding to the senses and it can focus on revising and storing memory. Also, it stands to reason that if you don't get enough sleep, you're too tired to think straight, much less remember 100 names and memorize a magazine.

Okay. Eat nutritious foods, drink plenty of water, and get some shut-eye. Anything else?
Women who are reaching the age of menopause should consider hormone replacement therapy (HRT). That's because estrogen production decreases in the years leading up to menopause, and estrogen seems to be instrumental in cognitive functioning. It may even help prevent or delay the onset of Alzheimer's disease, at least according to all the research I've seen. Women are at greater risk for Alzheimer's than men, and that risk increases after menopause. Scientists be-

lieve that hormone replacement therapy may lessen that risk.

Now let's talk about medication.

You mean there's something I can take to remember better? Why did I bother with this book?
No, I mean that some drugs can actually cause memory *loss*. These medications include certain tranquilizers, muscle relaxants, sleeping pills, and antianxiety drugs. Particularly problematic in this regard are the class of drugs known as benzodiazepines, including diazepam (Valium) and lorazepam (Ativan). Some high blood pressure medicines can also cause memory problems.

So if I need to take those medications, I can just resign myself to absentmindedness?
Not at all. First, you can work with your doctor to make sure you have the right dosage—enough to be effective, but not enough to produce undesirable side effects. If you do have memory problems while on your medication, use some of the memory tips in this book to counterbalance the effects.

> *We do not know the true value of our moments until they have undergone the test of memory.*
>
> **GEORGES DUHAMEL**

What about alcohol? I'm not suggesting drinking until I can't remember my own name. I'm talking about having a drink or two with friends.
Bad news. Even a little alcohol will affect your memory slightly, and the negative effect doesn't wear off in a few hours. Alcohol abuse, in the form of heavy drinking or alcoholism, is another story. Some of the worst cases of memory impairment are the result of alcohol abuse.

Smoking is probably bad for the old synapses, too, isn't it?
Well, it certainly doesn't help you when it comes to getting oxygen to the brain. Research has shown that people who smoke one or more packs of cigarettes a day have more difficulty remembering people's faces and names than nonsmokers.

And I suppose I have to lay off caffeine as well?
Good news there. Caffeine has a very positive effect on mental alertness. If you overdo the coffee, your nervousness may interfere with your memory, but if you use caffeine in moderation, it may actually help.

You say there are no drugs that improve memory. What about herbs and dietary supplements?
I'm not a doctor or a nutritionist. What I know about these things I've learned through reading, just like anyone else who is interested in the subject. I do know that claims about memory enhancement are made for all kinds of substances.

Do any of these things do any good at all?
That depends on who you ask. There have been hundreds of studies done on various natural substances. The only one that seems to have shown positive results in studies done in this country is ginkgo. It seems to have some effectiveness in people suffering from Alzheimer's disease. There are also reasons to believe it may be useful for anyone whose memory is impaired by aging. For one thing, ginkgo is a powerful antioxidant. For another, it increases blood circulation to the brain, as well as to all other parts of the body. So as with anything that acts like a drug, discuss it first with your doctor.

Has memory training been proved effective?
You bet it has. Just a couple of years ago, a meta-analysis—that's a study of the available research—looked at 31 studies

in which 1,539 healthy adults over 60 were taught mnemonic techniques. The results? Memory gains were larger among the trainees than in either the placebo or control groups. Score changes were greatest when memory-training sessions were short and took place in a group. And the best results were achieved *when subjects were younger*. Memory training was good for older people and even better for younger people.

Two other studies went even further and showed that the positive results of memory training were still apparent six months after the training ended and even *3 1/2 years* after training ended.

And the next time I read about the latest miracle memory enhancer?

Just read carefully. Look for controlled studies done on healthy people that show positive results. You never know. It could happen.

Okay, one last question. How young can memory training start?

Just about as early as you want. I've worked with children in individual classes who had been considered "slow" by their parents and teachers and have helped them memorize the states of the union in half an hour. Even children with learning disabilities can maximize learning with some knowledge of memory techniques.

Of course, I wouldn't subject any child to long sessions of memory training, or anything else. But there are a lot of fun memory games you can play, as you'll see in the next chapter.

The more you use your brain, the more brain you will have to use.

GEORGE A. DORSEY

EIGHTEEN

Memory Is Child's Play

If learning should be fun for adults, that goes double for children. The memory games I'm going to suggest will stimulate your kids, challenge them, and give their brains a workout. I'm also going to teach *you* how to teach *them* to beat the game of "Concentration."

Memory Game #1

Let's start with a game your children can play even before they can read or write. On the next page, you'd find a drawing of an empty room. The next time you go to the library or to your office, make some copies of the drawing, enlarging it if you can. Then, one rainy day when the kids can't go outside, give a copy to each child. Ask them to fill in whatever they'd like to put in the room—furniture, curtains, flowers, toys, whatever.

When the children are finished with their drawings, have them trade pictures. Ask them to look at the pictures carefully, noticing as many things as they can. Give the kids about a minute to study the pictures and then ask them to turn their papers over.

One by one, ask each child to tell what they remember

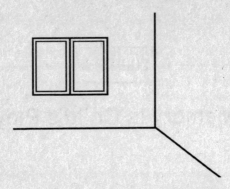

about the other child's drawing. You can make the game more fun by asking the child who created the picture to say whether the guesses are right or wrong.

Memory Game #2

This is a game you may have played when you were growing up. It's very simple, and the more people who play, the more fun it is. It's also a good game for the car. One person begins by saying, "Yesterday I went to the store and I bought . . ." and names anything from a box of cereal to a jet airplane. The next person repeats the sentence and adds another item. "Yesterday I went to the store and I bought a box of cereal and a diamond ring," for example. The game continues, with each person taking a turn and lengthening the list, until someone forgets one of the items.

Memory Game #3

This is really a variation on Memory Game #2. In this version, the first person chooses an item that begins with an A, and the game continues through the alphabet, in order: "Yesterday I went to the store and I bought an apple." Then, "Yesterday I went to the store and I bought an apple and a beach ball." The game continues with each person repeating all the items mentioned thus far and adding one more, until someone forgets an item. The interesting thing is that because the alphabet serves as a set of info-spaces, this game will probably go on quite a while. In fact, with older children, it may continue so long that the kids run into problems naming items that start with the right letter before anyone forgets anything.

The mind ought sometimes to be diverted that it may return to better thinking.

PHAEDRUS

Memory Game #4

This is a Method of Loci game. Ask a child to walk through the house and find ten places where she could put something. You might give her a few examples, for instance, "You could put something in the bathtub, couldn't you, or on top of the television?" Explain that she can choose any ten places, but she has to be able to walk from one place to the next, easily and in order. Have her literally make that trip from one place to another a couple of times.

Then ask her to sit down and *imagine* walking the same route. If she has trouble remembering all ten stopping places, have her go back to the actual places to remind herself.

Once she has her places firmly in mind, give her a list of ten unrelated items, such as the ones below. Explain that she can remember the items in order by *mentally* putting one item in each of her ten places and imagining what it would look like there. Then ask her to put the list aside and recite it from memory by retracing her steps *mentally*, "collecting" and remembering an item at each stopping place. See how much of the list she can remember.

Here are a couple of lists to start with:

ELEPHANT	BELL
BASEBALL BAT	TEDDY BEAR
CLOWN	GODZILLA
BANANA	DUCK
STAR	GOLDFISH
GRASSHOPPER	TRUCK
CASTLE	HORSE
FROG	STOP SIGN
CAR	LOAF OF BREAD
WITCH'S HAT	WALRUS

You can play this game with one child or with several. If you play with a group of children, don't make it a competition. The kids will have more fun if they're just trying to do their best.

Memory Game #5

This game is as old as the hills, but kids never seem to tire of it. Choose ten ordinary items—a pencil, a can opener, a coin, small toy, etc.—and put them on a table, tray, or large plate, covering them with a cloth. Tell the children that when you lift the cloth, they should look at the items in order to remember them later.

Give the kids about a minute to look, then re-cover the items and ask the children to write down all the items they remember. If you're playing with just one child, he can tell you what he remembers, without writing it down.

If the children you're playing with have already done Memory Game #4, change the items on the table and suggest that they use their "places" to help them remember the items. See if they do better than they did the first time.

Put another set of items under the cloth. Tell the children that, this time, you want them to think about the items in pairs. How can they do this? By associating the items, of course. If there's a can opener and a marble, for example, they might picture the can opener prying open a big marble. Encourage them to have fun by using their imagination to pair up the items in silly ways. After they write down their lists, see if making associations between the items boosted their memories.

Memory Game #6

A variation on Memory Game #5, this one can be done without any writing. Set out up to 20 items on the table, covering them with a cloth. Once again, lift the cloth and ask the children to look at the items for about a minute. Then replace the cloth and have the children close their eyes. Slip one item out from under the cloth and hide it from sight. Ask the children to tell you which item you took away.

Memory Game #7

This is a story game, very similar to the mini-movie technique you learned about in Part I of this book. In addition to exercising your child's memory, it stimulates creativity.

Give your child a list of six or seven unrelated items. Then ask her to make up a story that has all of the items in it. There are a couple of lists below to help you get started. To get the ball rolling, you may want to supply an opening sentence, such as the ones below.

giraffe
bridge
tree
duck
feather
river
bowl of soup
"Once upon a time, a giraffe named Wally went for a walk."

spaceship
monkey
mountain
baseball
snake
ice cream
shoes
"One day, a spaceship landed just outside town."

Memory Game #8

As you probably remember, "Concentration" was a parlor game long before it became the format for a popular television show. It's one of the best memory exercises you can do with children. To play the game, all you need is a deck of playing cards. You can use a regular deck, an Old Maid deck, or any other kind of cards you happen to have around.

For younger children, select fifteen pairs of cards—two fours, two kings, two sevens, and so on. Shuffle the cards and then lay them out face down in a grid that's six cards across and five cards down. Each player gets to turn over two cards at a time. If the two cards match, the player picks them up and takes another turn. If the cards do not match, she turns them back over and the next player takes a turn. The object of the game is to concentrate on the placement of the cards as they're revealed, to help match up the cards when it is your turn.

Now to beat the game, use this memory technique: teach an older child the info-spaces from 1 to 30. Then when a card is turned over, she can associate the info-space image with the card. For example, if a king is in the sixth space on the grid, she can visualize a king wearing one huge shoe. Then, on a later turn, when she flips over a king somewhere else on the grid, she'll remember that the matching king is in the sixth space.

There are dozens of other memory games to play with children. In fact, most of the methods you've learned in this book can be turned into games that kids will find challenging and fun. If you teach your children the number/sound system, for example, they can talk in numbers or give each other sentences to decode. With a little encouragement, you can probably even get a kid to help you practice when you're working on the techniques yourself.

NINETEEN

Remember This

Well, this is good-bye. I hope you've had fun and I hope your mind was challenged a little. You should take with you a new attitude toward memory and, with any luck, some techniques that will help you in your life and work.

Last joke of the book. How many memory trainers does it take to change a light bulb?

I'll bite. How many memory trainers does it take to change a light bulb?
At least two. Memory trainers can't do anything without associating.

Did you make that up?
Why?

Just answer me. Did you make that up?
Yes, I did. Did you like it?

Jon, I'm really going to miss you.
Yeah, well, as they say in the song, "Thanks for the memories!"

BIBLIOGRAPHY

Johnson, George. *In the Palaces of Memory*. New York: Alfred A. Knopf, 1991.

Keith, Jon. *Executive Memory Techniques*. New York: Dell, 1987.

Lorayne, Harry. *How to Develop a Super-Power Memory*. New York: Frederick Fell, Inc., 1957.

Middleton, A. E. *Memory Systems New and Old: Bibliography of Mnemonics 1325 to 1888*. New York: G. S. Fellows and Co., 1888.

Pressman, Alan H., with Helen Tracy. *Ginkgo: Nature's Brain Booster*. New York: Avon, 1999.

Turkington, Carol. *12 Steps to a Better Memory*. New York: Macmillan, 1996.

Yates, Frances A. *The Art of Memory*. Chicago: The University of Chicago Press, 1966.

FOR MORE INFORMATION

For more information about memory skill programs based on this book, contact:

Jon Keith
P.O. Box 731161
Ormond Beach, FL 32173
www.memorytrainer.com